PREACHING SERMONS THAT MATTER:
A Preaching Workbook
Based on the Dialectical Model
as Taught by Dr. Samuel Dewitt Proctor

ISBN: 979-8-9885340-0-6

Dedicated to the ministry and memory of a

"Friend to Preachers"

The Reverend Dr. Marvis P. May

And to my Brooklyn Pastor and Friend

Bishop Johnny Ray Youngblood

TABLE OF CONTENTS

ACKNOWLEDGMENTS

Writing is never a solitary effort. Thoughts are formed within the context of community and sharpened on the gavels of communal interaction. I begin by acknowledging the intentionality of my preaching forefathers, in particular my late father, Reverend Orenzia Bernstine, and my educational benefactor and pastoral predecessor, the Reverend Dr. Abraham Henry Newman. Early in my ministry they impressed upon me that preaching calls for thoughtfulness. Both men encouraged and included me in settings where the ministry and craft of preaching was academically considered. Dr. J. Alfred Smith, Sr. furthered their vision by modelling in my hometown of Oakland, California a preaching ministry that mattered beyond the safety of the sanctuary.

I'm also grateful for the three congregations, Olivet Baptist Church, Nashville, Tennessee; Mount Lebanon Baptist Church, Brooklyn, New York, and the Bethlehem Missionary Baptist Church, Richmond, California, who gave me nearly forty years of preaching opportunities. Whatever I have learned about preaching I learned from the loving and tolerant people of these three amazing congregations.

A special thanks to the School of Prophets, the Reverends Marcus Vanhook, Erika Godfrey, Marcus Mitchell, and the late Reverend Marvin Webb. Our weekly discussions on preaching encouraged and sharpened my attempts to preach sermons that matter. From the humble beginnings of the School of Prophets, I was invited to share with the Leadership Institute at Allen Temple (LIAT). LIAT expanded opportunities for me to share the lessons of my preaching journey, eventually allowing me to share in birthing the Bay Area Academy of Responsible Preaching (BAARP). Thank you, Reverend Dr. Brenda Guess, for your vision and trust. In Brenda Guess, I gained a treasured sister in the ministry of preaching and a friend. Thanks to the amazing staff and students of BAARP who gave me a context to shape and sharpen the contents of this workbook.

Again, I am grateful to Joyce Evans, my heroine in publishing. Joyce has made it possible for me to publish over ten books. That's pretty good for a young Black man who flunked English 1A and needed remedial English upon arriving on the campus of Bishop College, Dallas, Texas. A special appreciation for invaluable editorial suggestions from the dynamic Reverend Jini Kilgore Cockroft. If I ever become a good writer, it will be because I finally listened to Jini.

The Reverend Diana Becton, my dear wife, lover, soulmate, golfing partner, bowling buddy, music classmate, culinary tutor, traveling companion, thought partner, teacher, student, and beloved friend. Diana continues to unashamedly value and support my writing efforts. And to my wonderfully gifted, preaching daughter, the Reverend Kamilah Diarra Bernstine Bradley. Thank you, Deedah. Kamilah read the entire manuscript and gave invaluable critique and encouragement from the perspective of the Millennials.

FOREWORD

Today's world is rife with confusion. We are faced with glaring social disparities, shameful injustices, and national strife. In the wake of a global pandemic that shook the world to its core, it is crucial that contemporary preachers are adequately equipped with the skills that allow them to effectively encourage, inspire and nurture the lives of those who hear the gospel message. More than ever before, our world needs to see a beacon of light amid the looming darkness. Such a light is presented by the Reverend Dr. Alvin C. Bernstine in his latest book, *Preaching Sermons That Matter.* In a preaching workbook format, he casts that light in his preaching and teachings, an approach he's used at the Leadership Institute at Allen Temple, and throughout the country.

Dr. Bernstine is no stranger to the skill and artistry of preaching. He has more than thirty-five years of pastoral experience and is currently the pastor of Bethlehem Baptist Church in Richmond, California. He has graced the pulpits of churches across the country, including the National Baptist Congress and the historic Ebenezer Baptist Church in Atlanta, Georgia. Dr. Bernstine is staff instructor of the Pastor's and Minister's Division of the National Baptist Congress of Christian Education, National Baptist Convention, USA. Dr. Bernstine is the founder of The School of Prophets, a ministry to enhance effective preaching.

I first encountered Dr. Bernstine through his powerful preaching during Sunday morning worship at Allen Temple Baptist Church in Oakland, California. As guest preacher, he always provided a word that provoked deep thought and reflection. Not surprisingly, Dr. Bernstine would—without fail¾conclude his soul stirring sermons by taking the listener to the mountaintop of good news and hope. Dr. Bernstine mastered what Dr. Dante Quick appropriately called "thick preaching." The thickness was exemplified by Dr. Bernstine preaching sermons of substance, sermons that matter, and sermons that make a difference in the lives of the people.

A few years ago, I invited Dr. Bernstine to join the faculty of the Leadership Institute as our Homiletics Professor. It was here that the vision for a preaching academy was born. The academy would be a place where preachers could immerse themselves in learning experiences that focuses exclusively on the vital nuances of the preaching assignment, consistent with contemporary challenges and issues, yet grounded in the historical and theological traditions of the Christian Church.

Dr. Bernstine's creativity and leadership were instrumental in bringing a preaching academy –the very first to be offered in the country¾from vision into fruition. He presently serves as Dean of the Leadership Institute's Academy of Responsible Preaching. In this position, he leads a faculty of nationally renowned, and highly sought after preaching scholars.

In addition to being an outstanding preacher, teacher and scholar, Dr. Bernstine is a great author of ten books, including *Ministry in a Disaster Zone, Hope Us Lord, Parts 1& 2, Church Through the Roof,* and *a Ministry that Saves Lives.*

I am extremely excited to see this book come to the printed page. Dr. Bernstine, a fourth-generation Baptist preacher, brings his impressive experience to *Preaching Sermons That Matter*. In the workbook, Bernstine draws on the teaching and insights of Dr. Samuel Dewitt Proctor's Dialectical Preaching Model. Using this preaching methodology, the workbook offers the reader understandable step-by-step instructions on how to craft and shape compelling sermons that matter.

Dr. Bernstine declares that "preaching is work. Because of its subject matter and desired intent, preaching should not be easy, no matter how easy it may seem to come to some." Preachers using the dialectical model as presented by Dr. Bernstine, are encouraged to engage in critical thinking of the biblical text, and to take a holistic approach to theology and preaching.

Dr. Bernstine provides the reader with practical exercises that helps preachers to lean in and reflect on the readings thus developing their skills as they work through each step of the process of developing a sermon. This book also provides guidance in connecting with the audience and making sermons memorable.

Whether you are a preacher of many years, or just starting out on your preaching journey, you'll find this workbook an invaluable learning resource. *Preaching Sermons That Matter* is for anyone seeking to grow in their ability to preach the Word of God effectively and powerfully, and more importantly, to lead others into a deeper more intimate relationship with God.

Dr. Brenda Guess, Chancellor
Leadership Institute at Allen Temple

INTRODUCTION

Preaching as a Christian Practice

"Practices are those things *Christians people do together* over time to address fundamental human needs *in response to and in light of* God's active presence in the world." Thomas Long & Lenora Tubbs Tisdale, Teaching Preaching as a Christian Practice

During the experience of Jesus's Temptations, Satan ushers Jesus to the pinnacle of the Temple and offered up a seductive suggestion, "If you are the Son of God, throw yourself down from here, for it is written, He will command his angels concerning you, to guard you, and on their hands they will bear you up, lest you strike your foot against a stone (Luke 4:9-11, English Standard Version)." The state of preaching in America, particularly in Black America, painfully suggests that every Sunday preachers haphazardly jump from the steeple with the hope that God will send forth some angels to soar down and save them from the bad habits of ill-preparation. At least save them long enough to get to their whoop.

While facing the prospect of death from Stage 4 cancer, T. David- Gordon offered a blunt and sobering assessment of preaching in America. In his book, "Why Johnny Can't Preach"[1], Dr. Gordon observed that Johnny can't preach because Johnny /Jonetta[2] can neither read nor write. Johnny/Jonetta has allowed the seductions of technology to rob him/her of the capacity to engage texts with any appreciation for the literary richness of the biblical text. Consequently, his/her "addiction to the inconsequential" gets in the way of sermonic composition that consists of unity, order, or progressive movement. Sadder yet, many congregations are content with the current state of preaching and are quite amused with Johnny/Jonetta weekly taking entertaining leaps from the steeple.

The late Dr. Samuel Dewitt Proctor had little patience for "steeple jumping" preaching. Unlike T. David Gordon who courageously sounded the alarm, Dr. Proctor dedicated his life to saving preachers from ill-fated sermons. From the treasures of a remarkable preaching journey, he offered invaluable solutions. He personally taught, mentored, and shared his life journey in the service of improving the preaching ministry. In 1994 he set in print the essential elements of his preaching acumen and described in detail his approach to a sermon in the book, "The Certain Sound of a Trumpet: Crafting A Sermon of Authority."[3] His meticulous treatment of the Dialectical Model of preaching continues to serve us well as an invaluable preaching resource.

A huge part of my preaching testimony includes Dr. Proctor revolutionizing the preaching practices for so many of us. For some, our preaching may have been faring well, but Dr Proctor's presentation of the Dialectical Model radically improved our effectiveness. Like a gourmet cook's special recipe, the Proctor Model gifted us with a step-by-step process of consistently producing sermons worthy of public consumption. I was blessed to be part of the final cohort of 100 Doctor of Ministry students who were privileged to

---

1 T. David Gordon, Why Johnny Can't Preach: The Media Has Shaped the Messenger, (P & R Publishing, Philipsburg, NJ, 2009.
2 I add Jonetta in a clumsy attempt to be inclusive. T. David Gordon does not use Jonetta.
3 Samuel Dewitt Proctor, The Certain Sound of a Trumpet: Crafting A Sermon of Authority, (Judson Press, Judson Press, Valley Forge, PA, 1994)

sit at his feet at United Theological Seminary, Dayton, Ohio.[4] After my very first exposure to the Proctor Model, I immediately began a decades long journey of sharing what I believed to be a powerful approach of preaching sermons that matter. The Proctor approach to the Dialectical Model literally transformed my preaching testimony. (I haven't kept count, but hopefully I've impacted a few preachers through my feeble attempts to practice and my passionate efforts of teaching what I believe to be an effective approach to preaching.)

Dr. Johnny Ray Youngblood, one of the first Samuel Dewitt Proctor Fellows at United Theological Seminary, shared a personal experience of how impactful Dr. Proctor was on his life and preaching ministry. In the prophetically powerful book, "Upon This Rock: The Miracles of a Black Church,"[5] he shared an interesting preaching preparatory practice. He referenced a part of his sermon preparation of repurposing the folding board used in laundered shirts. (Repurposing was probably not the term he used.) On one side of the folding board, he would write out the sermon's proposition, thesis, antithesis, relevant question, and synthesis. On the other side, he would write out the sermon's outline and other pertinent notes, potential illustrations, and sermon ideas.

In a recent conversation with Dr. Youngblood, now Bishop Dr. Johnny Ray Youngblood, he reminisced how his folding board usage were influenced by the late Reverend Dr. William Augustus Jones. Dr. Jones carried envelopes within his inside suit jacket pocket to capture the elusive musings of his masterful preaching thoughts. Dr. Youngblood, a protégé of Dr. Jones expanded the envelope to the folding board. He repurposed the folding board as the workspace for developing sermon ideas. Dr. Proctor, who lived the early days of his life in the recovery phases of the Great Depression, practiced similar frugality. A part of his frugal practices, along with re-soling shoes multiple times, was to reuse any and every resource to jot down sermon thoughts and ideas. I recall flying on an airplane with Dr. Proctor and witnessed him scribble out sermon ideas on salvaged hotel note pads. I am almost certain that during Dr. Proctor's amazing preaching journey he, too, repurposed many folding boards. I've used folding boards, envelopes, hotel scratch pads – you name it, I've used it because sermon thoughts can be fleeting.

I am acutely aware of many preachers who never write out anything, pre-sermon or otherwise. My brilliant editor, Dr. Jini Kilgore Cockroft, gently convinced me that very few know anything about a folding board, but as Sir Francis Bacon once said, "Reading maketh a full man; conference a ready man; and writing an exact man."[6] This workbook is intended to aid preachers in the writing of sermons, or at least the essential sermon components. It is my offering of a folding book, or scratch pad-like assistance in helping preachers capture sermon ideas and then frame them in an effective methodology. Hopefully the process offered will assist in the difficult work of preachers becoming more exact. Currently the widespread use of pads and computers dispense with such frugal practices as repurposing folding boards or salvaged hotel note pads. Nevertheless, I want to offer a workbook for preaching based on the Proctor Model that I've employed for the last thirty-plus years. In a sea of incredible books on preaching, and the dynamics thereof, I humbly submit for consideration a Preaching Workbook that I believe assists in the effort to

---

4 The last Samuel Dewitt Proctor Doctor of Ministry Cohort graduated in 1995. The late Reverend Charles Booth served as his assistant.
5 Samuel G. Freedman, Upon This Rock: Miracles of a Black Church, (Harper Collins Books, New York, NY, 1993)
6 Sir Francis Bacon his essay "Of Studies" (1597)

preach sermons that matter. In this workbook I provide step-by-step my experiences and understanding of the Proctor Dialectical Preaching Model.

To be sure, others may view Dr. Proctor's preaching approach differently. Thankfully Dr. Proctor's mind, heart and ministry was vast enough to impact and encompass us all. I am also mindful and appreciative of other homiletical approaches, and especially sensitive to those used among marginalized communities, i.e., Womanist Preaching.[7] However, I believe the Proctor Dialectical Model remains a powerful tool for sermon development.

---

7 Dr. Donna Allen, the first black woman to receive a Ph.D. in Homiletics at Vanderbilt Divinity School, brilliantly espouses the Womanist Preaching approach. The late Katie Cannon also pioneered Womanist Preaching. Dr. Renita Weems continues to brilliantly practice and preach from a Womanist perspective. Additional sources from the Womanist perspective are included in bibliography.

HOW TO USE THIS WORKBOOK

Please be clear, preaching is work and most times it is hard work. Because of its subject matter and desired intent, preaching should not be easy, no matter how effortless it may seem to some preachers. The subject of preaching is always God, the things of God, and how the things of God matter to the ever-changing strategies of evil to conquer the human soul. Preaching seeks to provide a counter-narrative to the endless cycles of anti-faith, anti-love, and anti-human drama. For one, preaching's desired intent is to confront sinful, or broken human beings with the good news of God's incomparable love as expressed in a Crucified-Resurrected Savior. Secondly, the task of preaching demands a commitment to challenge high tech minds with ancient texts. Any effort to effectively penetrate the technologically enhanced atmosphere of today's world is formidable and challenging. Thirdly, preaching is an arduous undertaking as it attempts to integrate the eternal with the momentary, the spiritual with the physical, and bring all that to bear upon the complex lives of people who are daily bombarded with an array of life concerns and attractive life options. Thus, a preaching workbook embraces the labor of preaching and the specific work involved in producing a sermon worthy of people's time and attention.

As a workbook, it is my hope to offer specific rhetorical and literary objectives that enable the preacher to work on a process of consistently crafting sermons that matter. More specifically, the purpose of this workbook is to offer step-by-step suggestions on the usage of the Proctor Dialectical Model to preaching. By following the steps provided the workbook aims to offer preachers, and even lay people tasked to speak in church, a systematic approach to preparing sermons and or Bible-based lessons. Beyond my undying love and appreciation for Dr. Samuel Dewitt Proctor, my motivation for preparing the workbook is a response to confronting preacher after preacher, most who possessed no specific preaching methodology, at least not one he or she could articulate. As I embrace the sage age of life, what I'm offering is somewhat of a testimony. Like all testimonies, mine reflect a passionate desire to share something that has made a profound difference in my life and ministry. After preaching for nearly 50 years, (47 to be exact), I'm sharing a model that I'm fully committed to and can articulate. This model has allowed me to become a better preaching practitioner and homiletical clinician. In other words, because of the Proctor Dialectical Model I better practice preaching and more clearly understand what I'm doing while I'm doing it, as well as provide critical assessments of the sermon dynamics of others.

This workbook is my articulation of the Proctor Dialectical Model. It offers a methodology, if used well it assures that the preacher's sermon possesses homiletical integrity and thoughtful development. In the workbook I explain each element of the dialectical approach and suggest specific steps by how each element can be developed. The workbook format allows the student preacher opportunity to work out each element separate as he or she works toward the completion of the whole sermon. Clearly the pages of the workbook space limit the number of opportunities to work out a sermon within it, yet the ideas provided can be used endlessly. I am also mindful that good homiletics does not exclude or minimize good exegesis. When used well the Proctor Dialectical Model powerfully assists the preacher in nuancing the dynamic possibilities within the biblical text by its creative usage of tension. Tension stretches, expands, challenges, and modifies. Preaching should stretch us, expand our perceptions, challenge our pet assumptions, and modify how we show up in the world.

A major assumption for pulling together my thoughts on Proctor's Dialectical Model is my dogged belief that most preachers do want to preach well. Very few preachers who I have met were completely indifferent about what they would say on Sunday morning. Most preachers truly want what they say to mean something to the people who come with their own set of expectations. Preachers want their sermons to matter, and sermons ought to matter! They ought to matter to God. They ought to matter to oneself. Yes, and sermons ought to matter to the people. To those of a social activist bent – sermons ought to matter when confronting the ever-existing manifestations of evil and injustice.

The workbook is organized sequentially, beginning with a brief introduction of Samuel Dewitt Proctor. I consider his life to be so incredible that it deserves to be mentioned, especially in a workbook responding to his preaching acumen. My unwavering belief in the connection between preaching and prayer motivated me to take a risk and begin the workbook process with an offering of memorable quotes on preaching and prayer. Effective preaching thrives within the prayer environment cultivated by the preacher's prayer life. I offer undying gratitude for the preaching brothers and sisters who shared personal thoughts and quotes on preaching and prayer from the rich treasures of their preaching experiences. On a workbook sheet, questions are asked to focus and sharpen your responses as it relates to preaching and prayer. The condensed richness of the section on Preaching and Prayer can be done repeatedly as a pre-preaching exercise. In fact, I recommend it as a contemplative template for enriching one's preaching life.

I then offer a definition of the Dialectical Model, inclusive of what I consider both its pros and cons. A brief section on sermonic structure follows because sermon structure matters. How we preach is just as important as what we preach. The Proctor Model is introduced, and each component is elaborated upon. At the conclusion of each section, beginning with the section on Preaching and Praying, questions are asked, and suggestions given. The workspaces give student-preachers an immediate opportunity to react and interact with the workbook and test the veracity of the lesson offered.

To better appreciate the workbook, I urge you to read the introductory sections about Dr. Samuel Dewitt Proctor, the Dialectical Model Defined, and prayerfully consider the many ageless thoughts on preaching and prayer. Understanding the brilliance of Dr. Proctor and the thinking behind the Dialectical Model allows one to better appreciate the process of using the dialectical approach.

In the sections detailing the specific components of the Dialectical Model, I strongly recommend that each section be worked out separately and viewed as a process to an end. Like learning a musical instrument, one note, one key, and one octave at a time and then comes the song. For the workbook, that means the Proposition, the Antithesis, the Relevant Question, the Synthesis, and then comes the sermon. For each subsequent sermon attempt, the student-preacher is encouraged to work through the whole process, working out each step before moving on to the development of the next sermon idea. No matter how many sermon ideas we might ponder and possess, we can only preach one sermon at a time.

As a workbook, I aspired for it to be interactive. To that end I intersperse the book with "workbook" space as an opportunity for readers/student preachers to "work out" the development of the Dialectical

Model, as well as "think out" personal reflections on preaching. Two very important chapters are provided: one on Didactic Preaching for a Pandemic Stricken Church and another on Resurrection-Minded Preaching. Both chapters delve into critical aspects of preaching sermons that matter. In addition, I included an Appendix. Within the Appendix is a brief Greek lexicon on preaching words; suggested points on what I call "Juicing the Sermon," and some tried suggestions on the development of the Introduction, Body of the Sermon, Conclusion, and the Celebration.

The Appendix also includes a special section on a homiletical template for preaching eulogies, entitled, "Preaching Eulogies that Matter." I accredit Dr. Amos Jones, Jr. of Nashville, Tennessee for modelling a powerfully pastoral model for preaching eulogies. His uncanny ability to integrate a deceased person's life into the biblical text continues to shape and inspire my eulogistic efforts. As a seminarian at Vanderbilt Divinity School, I was privileged to witness Dr. Jones's preaching genius. He remains for me a model of preaching excellence.

With no intended hint of personal modesty, what may be the most valuable resource of this work is the incredible Bibliography and Resource created and compiled by Dr. Frank Thomas. I am eternally grateful to Dr. Thomas for graciously sharing from the wealth of his academic rigor. He represents what I consider a national treasure to the preaching academy. As Director of the only Ph.D. program in African American Preaching in the world, his value to the Kingdom is inestimable. If you are interested in studying and contributing to the African American preaching experience, I highly recommend Dr. Thomas's program.[8] The bibliography provides a wealth of resources to enrich your preaching journey and enhance your preaching perspective. Use it! Use it well! Use it often!

Finally, while I will never label myself as a great preacher, I do take pride in being consistently thoughtful. After nearly forty years of serving as a Senior Pastor, preaching remains for me a source of joy and inspiration. I love to preach, and I love the challenge, the cadence of sermonic preparation, and the entire process of developing a sermon idea. My love and joy of preaching has largely come from using the Proctor Dialectical Model to forge out sermon ideas. Few things satisfy me more than developing a great sermon idea. I pray you find and experience a measure of joy on your preaching journey, as have I through the use and application of this impactful preaching model.

If your preaching journey has led you to this book, I appreciate you giving it an opportunity to interact with your preaching. I further appreciate you believing enough in me to purchase the book and consider applying its principles to your preaching endeavors. May the Kingdom be expanded through the preaching of the Gospel. In the words of my dear friend and brother, Pastor Emeritus, the Reverend Dr. Edward L. Branch, "Preach strong!"

---

8 Frank A. Thomas, PhD, Director of the PhD Program in African American Preaching and Sacred Rhetoric and the Nettie Sweeney and Hugh Th. Miller Professor of Homiletics at Christian Theological Seminary, Indianapolis, Indiana.

INTRODUCING

DR. SAMUEL DEWITT PROCTOR

"One of the most important decisions you will make as a preacher is who you choose to be your mentor(s)." *—Samuel D. Proctor*

"No one present here today will ever meet another Samuel Proctor in your lifetime." Those were the opening words delivered by the late Reverend Dr. Gardner C. Taylor during Samuel Dewitt Proctor's eulogy, at the Abyssinian Baptist Church, NY, NY. Given the wide range of ages in the audience, I thought those remarks to be sermonic hyperbole, and not an assertion for serious contemplation. When stated, I was 45 years old and believed I had much more to learn and many more people to meet. However, the facts of his words remain true, if only for me.

As I turn the corner into more than seven decades of life, forty-seven lived in the preaching ministry, I'm somewhat taken by the fact that many of today's preachers know very little about Samuel Dewitt Proctor, or his dialectical approach to preaching. It appears the dizzying changes of the last twenty-years, accentuated by 24-hour news tickers and hyper social media; the ever rushed 21st Century preachers overlooked the impact of Dr. Proctor's preaching as many raced to the irrelevant sound bites echoed in today's pulpits. Many preachers have hung their homiletical hats on the idea of "Expository Preaching," although not always true to the practice of Expository Preaching.

It might be helpful to join Dr. Proctor on his evolution from biblical literalist to "understand that the Bible did not create God, Jesus or the Holy Spirit in the church. These were all realities before a single line was ever written by anyone. The Bible is a record of the events, not the events themselves, and the recording of the events was a process subject to human fallibility and human perceptions. But God is real, Jesus lived, and the Christ of faith lives still, and the Holy Spirit is here, both then and now."[9] However, from what I've heard, the results from many so-called expository preachers often lift ideas from the Bible but miss completely the critical essence of the Bible. Too many who claim to engage in expository preaching completely overlook the socio-political realities from whence the text emerged. In too many sermons the Exodus Story is spiritualized, and the trauma of the Babylonian Exile muted and domesticated. Rome's oppressive exploits and its impact upon the New Testament is silent. Rarely do I hear any so-called expositors mention anything about the oppressive barbarism surrounding much of the biblical text, leave alone how we might connect the Bible's witness to the oppressive pain of the Black experience in America.

By ignoring the social and cultural realities of the Biblical text, much of what parades as Expository Preaching fails to preach "the Bible." This is unfortunate because many of these brothers and sisters are brilliant, creative, and amazing cultural savants. Yet, the socio-political world of the Bible is often silent, robbing God's people of a perspective such as that articulated by the late Howard Thurman in the classic, "Jesus and the Disinherited."[10]

---

9 Samuel Dewitt Proctor, *My Moral Odyssey*, (Judson Press, Valley Forge, PA, 1989) p. 65.
10 Howard Thurman, *Jesus and the Disinherited*, (Beacon Press, Boston, MA, 1976).

Samuel D. Proctor never dabbled in sermonic trivialities. He seized upon the socio-political world of the Bible and effectively bridged it into the present age. His ministry served as a powerful social bridge during the early days of the Civil Rights Movement. Likewise, he understood that "an awful lot of dishonesty goes on when the preacher pretends not to know the chasm that exists between the worldview of the first century and the twentieth century or twenty-first – and the people pretend there is no chasm."[11] Adam L. Bond correctly characterizes Dr. Proctor as "The Imposing Preacher."[12] Utilizing the dialectical model he created the tension needed to keep the Bible relevant, interesting, and inspiring. Interestingly, his preaching approach has not received the homiletical attention our pulpits desperately need, nor its imposing impact prophetically bearing upon our sermon sensibilities.

Anyone who ever heard Dr. Proctor preach or speak inevitably learned something about his life story. He generously, but tactfully, used his own life-story as powerful illustration material for a biblical truth he was expounding upon, or a moral lesson being considered. For instance, in the sermon, "Standing at the Scratch Line," Dr. Proctor gives testimony to how family, church, and community gave him "blessings he never earned." He used the sermon to provide a platform where he "invited" us to learn about his beloved grandmother, Hattie Ann Fisher Proctor, formerly enslaved, yet she received a college degree at Hampton Institute. He proudly shared how Grandmother Hattie commanded and demanded the proper use of language and had a life-long impact upon his life. She served as a sort of Language Patrolperson within the Proctor family, something many of our families could benefit from today.

Within the sermon we learn about his humble upbringing in Norfolk, Virginia. We meet Herbert Proctor, his violin playing father, who taught the family four-part harmony. We are introduced to his mother Velma, a faithful and committed homemaker. As a prodigious child, he skipped three grades, graduated from high school at 15. He never considered himself as "privileged. Yet, unlike many of the young men in his neighborhood, Dr. Proctor understood the graciousness of his family, church, and community. He was privileged! He was privileged to be blessed with what he called "a moral incubator"[13] that provided him with certain social advantages.

Upon graduating from Booker T. Washington High School in Norfolk, Virginia, he took advantage of a music scholarship to attend Virginia State College. He played the saxophone and joined a jazz band and pledged Kappa Alpha Psi. Upon graduating from Virginia State, he attended the U. S. Naval Apprentice School receiving training as a pipefitter. However, pipefitting failed to capture the fertile and engaging mind of young Samuel, so he abandoned that effort and enrolled in Virginia Union University, where he met his wife, Bessie Tate.

The promptings of the call to Christian ministry, along with intellectual curiosity led him to Crozer Theological School, where he was the only black student in his class. However, at Crozer he attended the Calvary Baptist Church and came under the impactful influence of the Reverend Dr. J. Pius Barber. Years later I learned of the depth of Dr. Barber's impact upon Dr. Proctor's ministry, life, and person. The gravel tone of his voice could be traced to the gravelly voiced intonations of J. Pius Barber. Dr. Barber was

---

11 Op. cite, The Certain Sound of the Trumpet, p. 45.
12 Adam L. Bond, The Imposing Preacher: Samuel Dewitt Proctor and Black Public Faith, (Fortress Press, Minneapolis, MN, 2013)
13 Samuel Proctor, My Moral Odyssey, (Judson Press, Valley Forge, PA, 1989) pp. 19-33.

among those who engaged Dr. Proctor at the "Scratch Line!" It was Proctor's encounter with Dr. Barber that blazed a trail for many remarkable Black students to follow who attended Crozer and augmented their seminary time under the attentive tutelage of Dr. Barber. The list would include the Reverend Drs. Martin Luther King, Jr., William Augustus Jones, Amos Brown, Jr., Marvin McMickles, and many others.

Dr. Proctor's insatiable intellectual appetite led him to Yale, and eventually to Boston College where he would receive a Ph.D. in Theology. As a student and mentee of Dr. Proctor, he shared with me how he learned the dialectical approach to preaching. As a young theologian, struggling to connect the insights of higher education and biblical criticisms with the immanent challenges of Black life, he became disillusioned and uncomfortable with the preaching approaches practiced in most black churches. Moreover, the rigors of higher criticism and literary criticism had essentially ripped apart the Bible of his Huntersville religious experienced. One day he ran across an article written in 1918 by Harry Emerson Fosdick that restored his faith and steadied his ministry aspirations.[14] He recalled how he would leave the Black church experience on Sundays and rush home to hear the preaching of Dr. Harry Emerson Fosdick, Pastor of the Riverside Church, New York.

As he listened to Dr. Fosdick bring the Bible to bear upon the critical issues of that time, he noted not only the relevancy of his messages, but the rhetorical particulars of his preaching approach. Dr. Fosdick would state a proposition, develop a thesis, provide a powerful antithesis, raise a relevant question, and resolve the tension with an inviting synthesis. Dr. Proctor would later describe: "On his weekly radio programs Dr. Fosdick went after persons just like me. There was nothing superficial or simpleminded about his message. He was dead serious, and he probed into my doubts with penetrating thoroughness. He swept every corner of doubt and confusion clean with wide long strokes from the witness of literature, history, biology, astronomy, and the Bible."[15]

However, it was Dr. Fosdick's commitment to, and execution of, the dialectical approach to preaching that set the trajectory for Dr. Proctor's preaching life. The dialectical approach would not only shape his remarkable preaching ministry, but also serve to make him one of the most sought-after lecturers and commencement speakers in America. During my tenure in Nashville, the USA Today cited Dr. Samuel Dewitt Proctor as the Number One speaker at commencement services.[16] He was more popular at colleges and universities than then President Ronald Reagan.

Dr. Proctor's life was legendary. At the scratch line of his existence, he literally became what the late Dr. Gardner Taylor highlighted at his funeral. He was someone unlike anyone we would ever meet again in our lifetimes. At 33, he became the President of Virginia Union, later became the President of North Carolina, A.T. & T, at the same time the Reverend Jesse Jackson was the quarterback of the football team and the Student Body President. So impactful was Dr. Proctor's life upon Reverend Jackson that at Dr. Proctor's funeral, he stated, "He lived his whole ministry life trying to make Dr. Proctor proud." Upon an invitation to speak at Crozer, Dr. Proctor met young Martin Luther King, Jr., and a mentor-mentee relationship was

---

14 Ibid. pp.75-76.
15 Ibid. p. 75.
16 The article was written in the USA Today sometime during 1984 – 1988. Adam L. Bond writes on this experience in his book, The Imposing Preacher: Samuel Dewitt Proctor and Black Public Faith, (Fortress Press, Minneapolis, MN, 2013).

birthed. During the Montgomery Boycott, Dr. King invited Dr. Proctor to speak, and he raised money in support of the Greensboro sit-ins.

He later served as an Associate Director of the Peace Corps, which enabled him and his family to move to African for a season. Dr. Proctor was sought out by several U.S. Presidents as a mediator for Blacks during Civil Rights negotiations. He, indeed, stood at the "scratch line" during pivotal moments in United States history. As a student at Bishop College, I was assigned to transport guest preachers to the L. K. Williams Minister's Institute. Among those celebrated guests was Dr. Samuel Dewitt Proctor. At that time, I didn't know the magnitude of his person and personality. Yet, I was honored to drive him and the late Dr. Miles Jones to the Institute's proceedings. Both he and Dr. Jones humbly stayed on the campus during their visit.

Dr. Proctor would later befriend me and become my preaching mentor. "Bernstine, my main man!" he would warmly greet me. (I truly loved to hear him endear me in such a way.) When he accepted the assignment as Visiting Professor of Preaching at Vanderbilt Divinity School, Nashville, Tennessee, I was privileged along with Dr. Forrest Harris, to pick him up from the airport and transport him to his commodious lodging provided by Vanderbilt University. It was during his time at Vanderbilt where I became a life-long student of Proctor and attended every class he taught. On days when he was absent from class, a bubble-gum chewing, jean wearing young student from Shreveport, Louisiana, Joseph Warren Walker, III, (now the Presiding Bishop of the Full Gospel Baptist Fellowship), would set up tape recorded lectures for Dr. Proctor's class. All the enrolled students sat attentive for the two-hour sessions, riveted to the rich wisdom of Dr. Samuel Dewitt Proctor.

The late Marvis P. May, a classmate of mine at Bishop College would later submit my name to be invited into the Samuel Dewitt Proctor Doctor of Ministry Fellows. As fate would have it, I often travelled on the plane with Dr. Proctor as he commuted between Dayton, Nashville, and New York. He could have easily flown First Class, but his humility and frugality seated him in coach right next to me.

I shall never forget receiving the honored invitation to share in the book signing of his memoir, "The Substance of Things Hoped For." Upon arriving at a high-rise apartment on Park Avenue, an elevator attendant escorted me to a penthouse. I had only seen such privilege on television, or on the movie screen, so my cultural uneasiness was on full display. However, when I walked into the cavernous luxury of the Penthouse my anxieties dissipated. There dressed in a simple black suit, white shirt, and black tie was Dr. Samuel Dewitt Proctor being his most authentic self. "Bernstine, my main man!" He greeted me, as he held the celebrated space graciously engaging the noted host, editor, book agent, and a Who's Who group of New York's publishing community. That night I received an autographed copy of the book, plus a two-set cassette recording of the book, recorded by Dr. Proctor. (I recently converted the cassettes into cd's.) That's been over thirty years ago, and I've never had another such experience, because there's never been another person in my life like the late Dr. Samuel Dewitt Proctor.

GREAT THOUGHTS AND QUOTES ON
PREACHING AND PRAYER

Prayer involves an instinctive struggle for contact with reality; a period of calm and quiet in which one may listen to the divine whisper; an attitude of receptivity and expectancy which makes it possible for the soul to hear; an acceptance of the discoveries made in prayer, and a willingness to be guided by them in the daily life." —*Benjamin Elijah Mays*

I begin where I believe effective preaching is birthed. Effective preaching is the spiritual by-product of heart-filled praying. Preaching that touches the heart and stirs the dormant rumblings of the soul into redemptive action is conceived out of a passionate commitment to prayer. Dr. Proctor stood firm on the belief that "Praying is not asking. Prayer is putting oneself in the hands of God, at His disposition, and listening to His voice in the depth of our hearts."[17] The late Dr. C. A. W. Clark, whose preaching prowess is legend, impressed upon us would-be preachers that "praying and preaching go together." He, along with others, gave much attention to disciplining preaching with prayer.

I share from my bookshelf prayer aficionados like E.M. Bounds, Vance Havner, Leonard Ravenhill, and even Martin Luther. E. M. Bounds dedicated his life and ministry to evangelizing about prayer, and more specifically to prayer and preaching. Vance Havner, a beloved preacher-evangelist, delighted his readers with wit and wisdom on prayer. Contributing to this vital intersection of preaching and prayer are wonderful thoughts and quotes from personal preaching colleagues and friends. Their eager response to share testifies to the inextricable connection between preaching and prayer.

I am convinced that preaching and prayer are two essential elements of worship and spiritual growth. Most of our preaching takes place within the context of worship with the goal of facilitating some concrete, but not always measurable, expression of spiritual growth. When these two practices are combined, they have the potential to create a powerful and transformative experience for both the preacher and the congregation. "Prayer is not just a personal practice. It is also a communal one. We must pray together as a community, lifting up the concerns and struggles of preaching."[18] Preaching that does not transform the preacher is preaching void of the personal interaction of the preacher with God in prayer. Thus, I underscore the necessity that preaching and prayer go together and inextricably enhance one another's effectiveness. Preachers need a rich prayer life, and preaching flows best when saturated in prayer.

At its core, preaching is the sharing of God's Word through a sermon or homily. The purpose of preaching is to communicate the message of the Bible and help the congregation understand how an ancient text applies to complexity of their lives. Prayer, on the other hand, is a conversation with God, through which we excuse ourselves from selfish obsessions and ego-centric proclivities. (That sounds like something Dr. Proctor would have said.) In essence, prayer provides a moment when we get out of God's way, as well as our own. Howard Thurman aptly states that, "The true purpose of prayer is to break down

---

17 Samuel Dewitt Proctor and William D. Watley, Sermons from the Black Pulpit (Judson Press, Valley Forge, PA, 1984)
18 Op, cite, Sound of a Certain Trumpet

the walls of resistance within us to God's holy and loving will." During those moments of sacred exposure, we express gratitude, ask for guidance, seek forgiveness, and avail ourselves to God's Word for that day and for that people. Dr. Proctor adds, "Praying is an act of resistance against the forces of oppression and injustice. It is how we tap into God's power to bring about change in the world."[19] When preaching and prayer are combined, the preacher is inviting God's presence into the message, allowing the Holy Spirit to guide the preparation, delivery, and the capacity of the listener to courageously respond to the message with an open and receptive heart.

My record testifies that I am totally committed to inclusivity, especially in language. Most of my current and best preaching colleagues and students are women, many who I believe represent some of the best pulpiteers of today's Black church. Hence, I've included in this section words and thoughts from preaching women. However, some of the following quotes include men who lived in a time of less gender sensitivity. To preserve the integrity of their quotes, the language of their time remains intact. I pray you can reimagine the language for our day and glean the power of these quotes as uttered in their day. As far as I know, the men whom I quote were neither racist nor sexist, but men of their time functioning out of the language of their time. Thus, I pray you are as understanding as I am trying to be. If not, feel free to modify as you see fit.

> "Preaching requires the presence both of God and the preacher for the word to become flesh, one without the other leaves the people empty."
> —Dr. Forrest Harris, President of American Baptist College, Nashville, TN

> "Preach with all your heart, but also pay attention to the hearts on the other side of the pulpit."
> —Dr. Claudette A. Copeland

> The devil will let a preacher prepare a sermon if it will keep him from preparing himself.
> —Vance Havner

> "Preach the gospel at all times, and when necessary, use words." —St. Francis of Assisi

> "Preach the gospel always, and sometimes use words." —St. Teresa of Avila

> The first step towards doing anything in the pulpit as a thorough workman must be to kiss the feet of the Crucified, as a worshipper, in the study. —Thomas Armitage

> "Prayer is the submission of our thoughts to God's reality." —Walter Brueggemann

> "Preaching should be seen not as a way of achieving individual spiritual enlightenment, but as a way of participating in God's mission of liberation and reconciliation." —Walter Brueggemann

> To pray well is the better half of study. —Martin Luther

> "Prayer is not a substitute for action; it is an action for which there is no substitute."
> —Jo Ann Robinson

---

19 Op. cite, Sermons from the Black Pulpit

There is no chance of fire in the pews if there is an iceberg in the pulpit; and without personal prayer and communion with God during the preparation stages, the pulpit will be cold.

—Alistair Begg

"The only safe place to stand is in the presence of God." *—Gwendolyn Prothro Rencher*

Praying makes the preacher a heart preacher. Prayer puts the preacher's heart into the preacher's sermon; prayer puts the preacher's sermon into the preacher's heart. *—E. M. Bounds*

Every preacher who does not make prayer a mighty factor in his own life and ministry is weak as a factor in God's work and is powerless to project God's cause in this world. *—E. M. Bounds*

The preachers who are the mightiest in their closets with God are the mightiest in their pulpits with men. *—E. M. Bounds*

A Christian without prayer is just as problematic as a church without prayer." *—Patricia Raybon*

Prophetic preaching awakens imagination and moves the human spirit to act. When coupled with prayerful contemplation space is created for hearers to see what is possible in themselves and the world by looking beyond problems to encounter prophetic solutions.

—David K. Brawley

"Every great work of God begins with prayer." *—Ann Voskamp*

"Prayer is not just a private act, it is a way of connecting with others, with the world, with God, and becoming part of a larger community of love and compassion." *—Howard Thurman*

"To pray is to take notice of the wonder, to regain a sense of the mystery that animates all beings, the divine margin in all attainments. Prayer is our humble answer to the inconceivable surprise of living." *—Howard Thurman*

"Prayer is not so much for God, as it is for ourselves. It's our way of sharing in his caring and creation." *—Maya Angelou*

"The best preaching was made of prayer, trouble and study." *—Apostle E. W. Wilcots*

A FINAL WORD: "Prayer and preaching are inextricably bound together. The preacher who fails to take prayer seriously fails to take preaching seriously. Therefore, as the scripture says, "What God has joined together, let no man put asunder." Prayer and preaching are so vitally connected until when the preacher fails to pray, he/ she is certain to fail to preach. I am convinced, beyond the shadow of doubt that if God cannot speak to you in your prayer chamber, he will not speak through you in your preaching." *—Dr. Joe Albert Bush, Bronx, New York*

WORKBOOK EXERCISE

"Preaching and praying go together. And what God has joined together let us not put it asunder."
–C. A. W. Clark

Producing a sermon presupposes meditation and prayer.

Reflect upon the preaching and prayer quotes and thoughts offered above.

1. Do any of the quotes speak to you?

_____

_____

2. How so?

_____

_____

_____

_____

_____

_____

_____

3. Have you a quotable saying on preaching and praying? If so, write it below.

_____

_____

_____

_____

_____

_____

_____

_____

_____

4. What role does prayer play in your sermon preparation?

_____

_____

_____

_____

_____

_____

_____

5. Write out five specific things you need God to do in your preaching.

_____

_____

_____

_____

_____

_____

_____

_____

_____

_____

Share your five things you need God to with someone you love and trust.

Note: This might best be with someone who loves you but who is not always impressed by you.

THE DIALECTICAL MODEL - "The Model"

"That dog will hunt." –Samuel D. Proctor

In over thirty-years of preaching and teaching the dialectical approach, it has become known among my students, mentees, and fellow preachers as "The Model." I believe Bishop Sean Teal coined the phrase. While serving the Olivet Baptist Church in Nashville, Bishop Teal was one of the first preachers of whom I shared the Model. Consequently, he has become without question an avid practitioner and homiletical proponent of the dialectical approach. As far as preaching is concerned, he stands out among the preachers raised in the San Francisco Bay Area as consistently prolific and profound. While pastor at the New Hope Baptist Church, Oakland, CA, he included in the weekly program the dialectical outline of his sermons. Many of my Bay Area homeboy preachers claim to know "The Model," yet when I hear their preaching, it's obvious their assumptions are unfounded. However, Teal's preaching acumen and creativity illustrates a masterful understanding of the dialectical approach.

Perhaps a definition and explanation of "The Model" would assist those who yet struggle with putting it into practice. Again, while I believe Dr. Proctor's own words on the dialectical approach to be definitive, maybe a Proctor disciple's understanding could be helpful for other aspiring students of "The Model." I often heard Dr. Proctor say, "Anyone can be original if he or she is ignorant enough." Thus, what I offer makes no claims of originality. I am merely re-presenting what was graciously handed to me.

THE MODEL DEFINED

In essence, the Dialectical Model is a homiletical approach to preaching that seeks to bring together two seemingly opposing or contradicting ideas to generate new insights and understandings. Dialectical thinking brings into conversation two opposing ideas, yet both are true. The Model is a derivative of the Hegelian dialect espoused by the German philosopher Georg Wilhelm Friedrich Hegel. Hegel's dialectal approach's impact upon Western thought continues in just about every arena of thought from politics, economics, behavioral sciences, and in most social sciences. The dialectical approach has proved invaluable in critical thinking and social activism. Hence, making it such a powerful tool in addressing the complexities of theology and hermeneutics.

Philosophically and technically, the dialectical approach involves a three-step process of thesis, antithesis, and synthesis, in which an initial idea or position (the thesis) is placed in contradiction or challenged by a counterargument (the antithesis). The tension between the thesis and antithesis provokes thought that leads to a new, or more comprehensive understanding or resolution (the synthesis). Dr. Proctor's use of the dialectical approach presents an incredible opportunity for preachers to exercise critical thinking while engaging the Bible in the sermon process. Utilizing the Dialectical Model assists in making preaching an exercise in intentional thoughtfulness, versus the simple-minded parroting of overused cliches and the hand-me-down theological assumptions dressed in cultural exhibitionism.

The Dialectical Model provides an approach where the preacher constructs a rhetorical framework where she or he engages in an argument beginning with him or herself. The ensuing argument is packaged in a way that further invites the congregation to engage in a process of critical thinking that provides a deeper thinking about the faith and the implications thereof. Faith is not simple. Life can be complicated, and the mysteries of God continue to challenge, prod, provoke, and befuddle. Utilizing the dialectical approach calls us to move beyond pet assumptions about faith and life, inviting us into Abrahamic dimensions of faith by leaving the familiar and following God into the life-blessings terrains of the unfamiliar. The dialectical approach also demands Jacob-like tenacity, where the preacher wrestles in the night of an idea until a morning-time proclamation emerges.

In my efforts to teach or share the Proctor Dialectical Model a few observations have been made about its strengths (pros) and weaknesses (cons). Beginning with the pros: The Proctor Dialectical approach to preaching invites and encourages critical thinking and thoughtful engagement with the biblical text. When the preacher utilizes dialectical thinking he or she engages more deeply with scripture and offers the congregation an invitation to do likewise. Such critical analysis of the biblical text when juxtaposed with real-life concerns stimulates a preaching experience more inclined to produce some identifiable action. It makes the sermon live and invites the hearers to do something about what has been heard.

Jesus's use of Parables is an example of dialectical genius. The Mustard Seed provides an obvious tension between the small and the large, or the humble and powerful. The Sermon on the Mount challenges many acceptable social norms by presenting a dialectical tension between weakness and strength, mercy and justice, individuality and community. Clearly the so-called Parable of the Prodigal Son disrupts conventional wisdom and social norms with the tension between rebellion and obedience, sin and redemption, justice and mercy. The preacher whose mental capacity welcomes an encounter with critical analysis finds the dialectical approach incredibly useful and rewarding. Likewise, the congregation eager to make faith live are open to opportunities to affirm the gospel in new ways. Sometimes the difference between a good a sermon and a bad one is in the depth of thought, or the lack thereof.

Secondly, the Proctor Dialectical Model encourages a holistic approach to theology and preaching. The thoughtful preacher gets an opportunity to integrate multiple disciplines into the sermon event. He or she is not limited by ordinary preaching constraints, but free to intellectually roam to make the sermon live where it needs to live. The opportunity for intellectual rigor to make the gospel relevant allows the preacher wide range in applying the sermon to contemporary issues and challenges. I personally take a multi-disciplinary approach to understand and proclaim the gospel. Good news should never be limited to theology, when people's lives intersect with multiple experiences of reality, i.e., race, sex, gender, and class..

For instance, sin is more than personal misbehavior. Sin shows up in social systems and political structures and policies, of which all can be addressed through holistic preaching. I was encouraged to read a Korean theologian's understanding of sin that exponentially broadened my perspective on sin.[20] Andrew Sung Park presented an Asian understanding of sin as "han, frustrated hope, the collapsed feeling of letting

---

20 Andrew Sung Park, The Wounded Heart of God: The Asian Concept of Han and the Christian Doctrine of Sin, (Abingdon Press, Nashville, Tennessee, 1993)

go, resentful bitterness, and wounded heart."[21] How incredibly expansive can the preacher talk about sin when understood to be a soul wound "caused by abuse, exploitation, and violence."[22]

I recently preached a sermon from 1 Peter 2:1-10, entitled, The Transformative Power of Stones. I was able to use Park's understanding of sin to better see and explain how a people hardened by abuse and oppression can be transformed into "living stones." Peter wrote to a people inflicted with soul wounds, who were harming one another. Hurt people, hurt people! However, as living stones, we have the responsibility to "proclaim the excellence of him who called you out of darkness into his marvelous light."[23] The Dialectical Model graciously invites and encourages holistic thinking.

Thirdly, the Proctor Dialectical Model is incredibly adaptive. One of the joys of witnessing Dr. Proctor preach was his sermonic versatility. He could preach a sermon and mesmerize an audience of intellectuals in a Divinity School Chapel and make the same sermon come alive in the sanctified walls of a storefront church. Without dumbing down, or being intellectually pretentious, Dr. Proctor demonstrated the Dialectical Model's relevance and accessibility to a wide range of audiences. The Dialectical Model gifts the thoughtful preacher with the homiletical quiver necessary to function in an ever-expanding pluralistic society.

In addition to the above strengths (pros) of the Proctor Dialectical Model, it possesses a couple of weaknesses, or challenges, to which I now address. My dear wife, Diana, who is a superb preacher and practitioner of the Model, helped me to consider that the Dialectical Model can be intellectually challenging. While I don't believe preaching is easy, nor is it supposed to be, the intellectual acumen needed for critical thinking challenges many. This is never more evident than when I witness students struggling with developing a proposition, or a thesis. Bringing one's racing and rambling thoughts under subjection to a single, declarative idea proves difficult for many. It is difficult because the Dialectical Model demands a level of intellectual and theological energy and discipline that many preachers lack, or have never cultivated. Preaching dialectically does not fit into the vernacular of the presumptuous thinking of hand-me-down religion.

When preachers are not predisposed to invest a high level of intellectual and theological energy into preaching, the Dialectical Model proves daunting. Unfortunately, many African Americans and other marginalized people suffer because of inadequate primary education. Unlike Dr. Proctor, not many of us were introduced to the classics, expected to quote Tennyson, or immersed in the thinking that shaped Western thought. Very few of us had a Grandma Hattie who expected and demanded the proper use of the English language. Consequently, the invitation to engage in critical thinking about the Bible, life, or preaching proves difficult.

The second weakness, or con to the Proctor Dialectical Model is it requires a significant investment in time and effort. The Dialectical Model is not for the lazy, nor the timid. Preaching sermons that engage life in the complex spaces where people live is demanding. Preparation and planning are significant and must be intentionally approached. Most serious teachers of homiletics suggest working on parts of the sermon

---

21 Ibid. p. 31
22 Ibid., p. 20
23 I Peter 2:9b, New International Version

each day of the week. For instance, develop the proposition on Tuesday (assuming Monday is a day off); on Wednesday, work on the antithesis; on Thursday shape the relevant question and synthesis, and on Friday write out the sermon. Admittedly, this might challenge bi-vocational preachers and pastors. Yet, doing something on the sermon each day of the week pays enormous dividends on Sunday. (I will speak again to this strategy later in the book in the Chapter, entitled, "Lining It Out.")

My hope for the workbook in your hands is that it provides an understanding and an approach to the successful use of the Proctor Dialectical Model. Just as the Bible possesses books and letters that were not written by the stated authors, but by students or even impacted communities, I'm proud to be a proponent of my preaching mentor, Dr. Samuel Dewitt Proctor. I earnestly believe that the preaching model of Dr. Proctor is worthy of a school of disciples who advance the excellencies of his effective approach to preaching.

I find it interesting that after twenty-years of the Samuel Dewitt Proctor Conference, where each year a stirring video clip is provided of him preaching and a thoughtful litany recited from his words, his preaching genius has yet to be explored. (A constant highlight for me is to make my way down to the opening plenary of the Conference so I can once again sit and listen to Dr. Proctor's voice.) I applaud the conference's leadership, influenced by the inimitable Dr. Jeremiah Wright, the superlative guidance of Dr. Ida Carruthers and the charismatic brilliance of Dr. Frederick D. Haynes, III. They all work hard to offer probing and powerful presentations that indeed capture the compassionate heart of Dr. Proctor. However, as an "OG" conferee of every annual Conference, I've yearned for a thoughtful conversation around the preaching model he so fervently espoused. During a time when seminaries are minimizing preaching, I believe the Seminarians in attendance would be intrigued by his dialectical approach.

My hope and prayer that I do justice to the genius of one of the most compassionate, intelligent, prophetic scholar-preachers birthed and shaped in the American Christian experience. His spirit lives in me and if my preaching has meant anything to anyone it's because of the impact on my life and ministry of Dr. Samuel Dewitt Proctor.

STRUCTURE MATTERS

The Dialectical Model essentially assists in organically processing the "idea life" of the sermon through an intentional structure. Sermons live when birthed out of great ideas. However, great ideas need structure to live beyond the ethereal domain of the mind. Good ideas go forth when packaged in an effective structure. Here are a few things I believe about good structure as it relates to preaching:

1. **Good structure** confirms and solidifies the preacher's grasp of the sermon's material.

2. **Good structure** helps the preacher emphasize a central idea, rather than dabble in several minor ones. The idea life of the sermon emerges best from a structure that gives life.

3. **Good structuring** encourages the preacher to know her or his target and not digress from it.

4. **Good structuring** results in good sermonic movement toward an appropriate climax that supports life.

5. **Good structuring** also results in a "balanced presentation," avoiding overloading and underloading.

Overloading occurs when one part of the sermon dominates and minimizes other parts of the sermon to the extent that the sermon becomes convoluted. An example is when one point, or part of the sermon is well-thought out, provocative and imaginative and the next part is noticeably not as thoughtful, less provocative, and lacking in imagination. Listening to a recent sermon I witnessed the congregation's enthusiasm for the sermon diminish after a strong first point was followed by four tepid ones. A great sermon was aborted because the sermon lacked balance.

Underloading occurs when one part of the sermon is minimized into being inconsequential, thereby reducing the sermon's potential. Here the example is the opposite of the above: one point, or part of the sermon lacks the substance, thoughtfulness, or imaginative input of other parts of the sermon. Like a bad movie where one character is highly developed, but little is known about the would-be supporting characters. Sermons need symmetry to hold the hearers' attention.

Good structuring helps the preacher's delivery by providing a natural flow that brings forth the preacher's personality. My daughter poignantly noted the incongruity of the often-used prayer, "Lord, hide me behind the Cross so that only Jesus is seen." Interestingly, John wrote, "The word became flesh and dwelt among us, and we have seen his glory, glory as the of the only Son from the Father, full of grace and truth."[24] Phillip Brook's words ring true, "Preaching is truth through personality." While no preacher should ever preach just to be seen, good structure allows the preacher's personality to emerge as a central witness to the integrity of the sermon.

Good structuring enhances the preacher's credibility with the audience by making the sermon more impactful.

---

24 John 1:14, New International Version

STRUCTURE HELPS SERMONS TO MATTER

The Dialectical approach to preaching gives the preacher a structured approach to sermon development and delivery. Using the Dialectical Model, we discover that sermons matter when structurally focused on four things. I offer four words to consider and encourage you to respond in the provided work spaces.

Declaring – the sermon needs to declare something!

RESPONSE: What does "declaring" something mean to you?

_____

_____

_____

_____

_____

Describing – the sermon describes why it is declaring what it is declaring!

RESPONSE: What does "describing" mean to you?

_____

_____

_____

_____

_____

Inquiring – the sermon needs to inquire about the relevancy of what it is declaring and describing.

RESPONSE: What does "inquiring" mean to you?

_____

_____

_____

_____

Suggesting – the sermon needs to suggest a response to the inquiry.

RESPONSE: What does "suggesting" mean to you?

_____

_____

_____

_____

_____

I'm proposing that the **Dialectical Model** shapes sermons that matter through the skillful use of four dynamic moves, statements, or sentences. The four sentences/statements/moves are as follows:

1. DECLARATIVE

2. DESCRIPTIVE

3. INTERROGATIVE

4. SUGGESTIVE

In Socratic language, the moves of the four sentences/statements/ are dialectically known as

The Proposition/Thesis - Declarative

The Antithesis - Descriptive

The Relevant Question - Interrogative

The Synthesis – Suggestive

AN OUTLINE OF THE PROCTOR MODEL

THE DECLARATIVE

What the Sermon Declares

The declarative sentence represents the Proposition, or the thesis.

The declarative sentence declares **what** the sermon is going to be about.

THE DESCRIPTIVE

The descriptive sentence represents the **antithesis.**

The descriptive sentence describes **why** the sermon has been declared as important.

THE INTERROGATIVE

The interrogative is the relevant question.

The interrogative asks why, how, or what faith responses are to be considered.

The interrogative sentence, which is a question, asks for the **relevance** of the sermon in the life of the believers. (According to Dr. Proctor, the relevant question begs to be answered!)

THE SUGGESTIVE

The suggestive is the **synthesis.**

The suggestive sentence provides suggested faith **responses** for believers to consider, and/or to incorporate into their lives.

Not every idea is big enough, encompassing enough, celebrative enough, probes deeply enough into our internal arrangements of values and priorities, or close enough to the vibrations of eternity hovering over us to claim the people's time in the name of a sermon. —*The Sound of A Certain Trumpet, Samuel A. Proctor*

I hold that a sermon should be heavy enough to mean something, but light enough to be carried away.

THE PROPOSITION/BIG IDEA/MAIN IDEA

"What the Sermon Declares"

If you ain't got no proposition, you ain't got no sermon neither. *—Isaac Rufus Clark*

The above quote was the homiletical battle cry of the late Isaac Rufus Clark, one of the most influential and colorful professors of homiletics in the Black church in the twentieth century. Dr. Clark taught preaching at the Howard University School of Divinity. He was an avid advocate that a sermon's life be predicated upon a strong proposition. He believed, as did Dr. Proctor, that the proposition platforms what the sermon is about. Proctor asserted:

> The proposition of the sermon says what the sermon is all about …
> It is the most important because it presents the main idea, the word that comes during communion with God in prayer.[25]

For a sermon to matter, it must be about something, and not about everything!

Most preachers struggle with clarity, not brevity. Therefore, many end up saying a lot about many things without being clear on anything. Consider further the proposition:

The proposition is a faith statement…

The proposition is also a positive and affirmative declaration.

> It is a sample of the preacher's total theology, an authentic "for instance" of the best answers the preacher has found to life's persistent and ponderous questions.[26]

> The proposition must be clear and of significant weight because it will expand, and further along in the outline will be enlarged and become the thesis of the sermon.[27]

> The proposition should be written down and kept before the preacher throughout the sermon's preparation.[28]

This is the most important statement within the sermon.

This statement will determine the life, and without it assures the premature death of the sermon.

This statement is the one that will guide and shape everything that is said within the sermon.

This statement will be the one idea that will be most repeated and remembered in the sermon.

This statement is the foundation upon which the entire sermon will be built.

---

25 Op. cite, *The Certain Sound of the Trumpet*, p. 33
26 Ibid., p. 34
27 Ibid., p. 41
28 Ibid, p. 51

PROPOSITION/THESIS AS A DECLARATIVE STATEMENT:

Declaration - A declarative statement directs the preacher and the listener as to what the sermon is about. It can be framed as the **BIG/MAIN IDEA.**

A declarative statement states a fact or an argument and conclusively ends.

Possibly the most common sentence type in the English language, declarative sentences are used when you want to make a statement. Whether the statement is a bold statement or a simple fact, the sole purpose of a declarative sentence is to give information. It always ends with a simple period. And if you'd like to see an example of a declarative sentence, you don't need to look any further. Every sentence in this paragraph is a declarative sentence.

THE DYNAMICS OF THE PROPOSITION/DECLARATIVE SENTENCE

The period, or full stop, marks the end of a *declarative sentence*.

A declarative statement sets forth a specific direction or thought pattern to follow.

How to Write a Declarative Sentence

Writing simple declarative sentences is a matter of following a simple writing formula:

Subject + Predicate

Declarative sentences always have a subject and a predicate.

SUGGGESTED STEPS TO SHAPING THE PROPOSITION:

1. Identify a key thought or word that is stated or suggested in the biblical text and/or an idea birthed through prayerful contemplation.

   NOTE: Ideas for sermons can come from thoughtful observations in the world, in the life of people, music, literature, history, or personal experiences.

2. Write down the key word or thought.

3. Identify how the key word or thought is functioning in the text for the original listeners.

4. Consider how the key word or thought might function in today's church.

5. What is the challenge in the word or thought?

6. Write out a trial sentence, or several trial statements, until one succinctly and clearly **declares** what you believe the sermon will be about.

   PLEASE NOTE! While the proposition informs the title/subject, it is not the title/subject! The title/subject announces the proposition.

THINGS TO AVOID WHILE PREPARING THE SERMON PROPOSITION

1. **Avoid run-on sentences**. Run-on sentences increase the possibility for sermonic chaos and audience confusion. Succinct and simple works!

   If there's mist in the pulpit, there's a fog in the pew. –Dr. Claybon Lee, Jr.

2. **Avoid verbatim repeating what is already in the text as your propositional sentence.** Being verbatim suggests either laziness or lack of imagination. God is a creative God. Dare to be creative!

3. **Avoid inquiries or using questions as your proposition.** Although I've witnessed seasoned preachers do extremely well raising questions in their propositions, it is quite uncommon. It's best to declare something rather than ask about something that perhaps you are the only one concerned about that something.

4. **As much as possible, avoid clichés, or common sayings, or verses from popular songs.** Sometimes they work, but most time they ring flat and demonstrate a lack of imaginative struggle. Cliches and songs might help us preach, but they need not be what we preach!

5. **Avoid plagiarism.** Plagiarism is stealing other people's thoughts and ideas without giving them credit. Preaching depends much upon the integrity of the preacher, and to steal other people's thoughts and ideas reduces the preacher's credibility. Give credit where credit is due!

AN EXAMPLE PROPOSITION

TEXT: Psalm 100:3c

TOPIC: The Sheep People

Proposition: The idea that drives this sermon is that **we are most likely to maximize our humanity when we are attached to the right identity, or who we know ourselves to be.**

MORE EXAMPLES:

- The Lord shepherds those who want to be shepherded (Psalm 23:1).
- There are specific places where the Lord can use our unique giftedness to provide an effective witness (Acts 1:8).
- Obeying Jesus always brings positive results (John 2:5).
- Submission places us in the best position to hear from God (Mark 1:9-11)

A WORKBOOK EXERCISE ON THE PROPOSITION

Use the following texts for practice in writing out a proposition.

TEXT: Psalm 23:1

PROPOSITION/THESIS: _____

_____

_____

_____

TITLE: _____

TEXT: Acts 1:8

PROPOSITION/THESIS: _____

_____

_____

_____

TITLE: _____

TEXT: John 2:5

PROPOSITION/THESIS: _____

_____

_____

_____

TITLE: _____

TEXT: Mark 1:9-11

PROPOSITION/THESIS: _____

_____

_____

_____

TITLE: _____

THE ANTITHESIS

What the Sermon Describes

We are under no obligation to preach great sermons, but we are obligated to wrestle with great ideas.

—Howard Thurman

THE DESCRIPTIVE STATEMENT

The descriptive statement represents the Antithesis.

Antithesis – the opposite of

The descriptive statement shapes the central reason why the sermon has been declared as important, and important enough to declare at this moment to this people.

ANTITHESIS – This statement/section provides a **description** of some key concern(s) within the world/text/church as to why the sermon is important enough to preach.

What makes this sermon important? …

The antithesis raises the need; the thesis answers it. *—Proctor*

According to Dr. Proctor, the antithesis addresses one or more of the following:

- an error that must be corrected
- a condition that must be altered; a mood that must be dispelled
- a sin that cries out for confession and forgiveness
- some ignorance that needs to be illuminated
- a direction that needs to be reversed
- an idolatry of worshiping that is corruptible
- some pain and hurt that awaits the balm of Gilead
- some lethargy that needs to be replaced.[29]

As a descriptive sentence/statement the antithesis prepares the minds of the listeners to hear the claims that will be presented throughout the sermon.

The antithesis insists that, "We really need to consider this because…"

Only the preacher came with that (the antithesis) in mind. It is the preacher's task to put it [the claims of the antithesis] into the minds of the listeners. *—Proctor*

---

29   Proctor. *The Certain Sound of the Trumpet.*

As a **descriptive** statement, the antithesis offers a **contrast** to the proposition.

It sets in "real life" the contrasting realities stated within the **proposition.**

The sentence containing the antithesis is a statement of **justification.**

It justifies what makes the truth of the proposition so **compelling.**

One can tell if the sermon's proposition is really strong by the quality of the antithesis it evokes.

—Proctor

The antithesis provides some clear description(s) of some obvious reality, or condition in dire need of transformation.

The antithesis as descriptive sentence/statement provides detailed information that allows the listener to form an image in his or her mind.

The better the description, the clearer the image.

The description is a statement of **support.**

The antithesis provides descriptive support for the **relevancy** of the sermon by inviting the listeners to consider the **validity** of what is being preached.

THE FIVE C'S OF A GOOD ANTITHESIS

I believe that the antithesis functions best when addressing issues that are:

Current –Through the lenses of the biblical text the issue can be considered as currently happening in the here and now.

Critical – The issue critiques the faith claims either within the self, shared belief systems, the church, or the society.

Concrete – The issue can be concretely observed, felt, or experienced.

Challenges – The issue challenges a matter intentionally, emotionally, socially, theologically, and intelligently.

Connects – The issue is brilliantly tied to the proposition in ways that **connect** the imagery of the biblical text to the lives of God's people.

SUGGESTED STEPS TO DEVELOPING THE ANTITHESIS

1. Locate a key word, image, or thought, within the text or the proposition that can be used to provide a contrast. The word, image, or thought usually has something to do with behavior that is anti-faith, anti-community, or anti-love.

   Write down the key word or thought.

2. Identify some ways in which the key word or thought is being played out in the world, the church, or even within the psyche of the community of faith.

   NOTE: It is often a theological matter being played out in the drama of human behavior.

3. Consider ways in which the matter being described diminishes who we are as people of God, violates community, or limits faithful living.

4. Write a trial sentence, or a number of trial sentences, until one provides a **powerful** and **undeniable description** that contrasts with the claim(s) made by the proposition.

5. Dr. Proctor's treatment on the Antithesis in the book, *The Certain Sound of the Trumpet* is invaluable. Please consult!

THINGS TO AVOID WHEN SHAPING THE ANTITHESIS

1. Avoid developing another proposition, or a new sermon idea.

2. Avoid forcing a concern that is unrelated to the text, or the proposition.

3. Avoid weakening the claim(s) made in proposition with trivialities.

4. Avoid inciting the congregation by using embedded bigotries, or long-standing cultural biases to score "stupid" points with the listening audience. Countless are the times when I've heard preachers exploit the homophobic inclinations of listeners to incite listener response to a sermon that was going no-where. Never dumb down to the base instincts of an audience!

5. Avoid self-focused illustrations to advance self-interests.

AN EXAMPLE OF A PROPOSITION AND AN ANTITHESIS

TEXT: Psalm 100:3c

TOPIC: The Sheep People

PROPOSITION: The idea that drives this sermon is that **we are most likely to maximize our humanity when we are attached to the right identity, or who we know ourselves to be.**

ANTITHESIS: What makes this message so powerfully relevant is that too many of us don't know who we are because many of us suffer from what the psychologists call "attachment disorders."

It's hard to get your identity straight when you lack healthy communal and social attachments.

OTHER POSSIBLE ANTITHESES

Israel's story reveals that there are those who behave as if they don't want to be identified as being shepherded by the Lord. Psalm 23:1

We waste precious time pursuing ministry experiences that don't identify us as the Lord's people.

Our most negative experiences are often the consequences of evil imposed upon us.

Our unwillingness to submit distorts our capacity to adequately identify with God.

A WORKBOOK EXERCISE ON THE ANTITHESIS

Use the exercise Propositions developed in the previous Workbook Exercise, to construct some possible antitheses, or descriptive statements.

Consider utilizing the **The Five C's to A Good Antithesis** and the suggested steps to the antithesis. Also pay attention to what to avoid.

TEXT: *"The Lord is my shepherd I shall not want" (Psalm 23:1).*

PROPOSITION: _____

_____

_____

TITLE: _____

ANTITHESIS: _____

_____

_____

TEXT: *"But you will receive power when the Holy Spirit has come upon you, and you will be my witnesses in Jerusalem and Samaria, and to the end of the earth"* (Acts 1:8, ESV).

PROPOSITION: _____

_____

_____

TITLE: _____

ANTITHESIS: _____

_____

_____

TEXT: *"His mother said to the servants, "Do whatever he tells you"* (John 2:5, ESV).

PROPOSITION: _____

_____

_____

TITLE: _____

ANTITHESIS: _____

_____

_____

TEXT: *"In those days Jesus came from Nazareth of Galilee and was baptized by John in the Jordan. And when he came up out of the water, immediately he saw the heavens being torn open and the Spirit descending on him like a dove. And a voice came from heaven, 'You are my beloved Son, with you I am well pleased'"* Mark 1:9-11, ESV).

PROPOSITION: _____

_____

_____

TITLE: _____

ANTITHESIS: _____

_____

_____

THE RELEVANT QUESTION

What the Sermon Interrogates

The relevant question interrogatively connects the sermon's proposition with the antithesis. It asks why or what must be done to resolve the tension created between the proposition and antithesis. When the relevant question follows the thesis and antithesis, hearers/believers experience a natural response that can be described as 'desired tension.' Dr. Proctor contends, "The Relevant Question is already asked in the minds of the hearers—whether the preacher ever gets to it or not."[30] I practice the Proctor Model of constructing a relevant question that either rises in my own mind, or as I anticipate what might emerge within the minds of the people.

THE DYNAMICS OF THE RELEVANT QUESTION

- It is a question that must be answered!

- It must be answered by the preacher.

- It must be answered by the text.

- It must be answered in the life of the listeners.

THE INTERROGATIVE/RELEVANT QUESTION

- This sentence is also a transition to the body of the sermon, or the major points of the sermon.

- This sentence supports and enhances the relevancy of the sermon.

- This sentence will provide you, as well as the listeners, with vital clues to the direction of the balance of the sermon. It is important that you, the preacher know where the sermon is headed, and for the people to know that the sermon has a specific direction. Neither preacher nor the people profit from sermons with no direction.

SUGGESTED STEPS TO THE RELEVANT QUESTION

- Connect the question to the world, or the historical/cultural setting of the text.

- Be clear on how the text supports the question.

- Make sure the question is a natural/organic consequence of the thesis and antithesis.

- Connect the question to the tension that was created in your own life/mind by the previous two statements, the proposition and antithesis.

- What is it that you feel needs to be resolved?

- Connect the question to the tension you anticipate creating in the lives of the believers/hearers.

- What tension or concern did you hope to create in the sermon?

- The tension/concern should be stated in the normal words of a question.

---

30 Proctor. The Certain Sound of the Trumpet.

- Use interrogative words such as, What? Why? How? Where? For what cause? From whence comes? etc.

- Try to make the question so compelling that it "begs" to be answered!

- Create the question in such a way that it makes the rest of the sermon relevant in the lives of the believers/hearers. Hence, it is called the Relevant Question.

THINGS TO AVOID IN DEVELOPING THE RELEVANT QUESTION

- Avoid forcing a question that does not connect with the text.

- Avoid forcing a question that does not connect with the proposition/thesis and antithesis.

- Avoid creating another proposition/sermon.

- Avoid complicating the process unnecessarily.

- Avoid using another text to create the question? Example: If you are preaching from John never answer by saying, "According to Mark."

EXAMPLES OF THE RELEVANT QUESTION

(These examples come from the texts offered in the previous examples.)

- What are the benefits of being shepherded by God? Psalm 23:1

- How do we embrace the particular places God calls us to serve? Acts 1:8

- What happens when we obey Jesus? John 2:5

- What might we experience through submission? Mark 1:9-11

THE SYNTHESIS
What the Sermon Suggests

This sentence/statement is, at best, suggestive. Being a preacher too easily seduces us into narcissistic delusions that cause us to believe our words and thoughts stand true for all circumstances, for all time, for all people, and in every situation. Such delusionary claims to absolutism inhibit personal growth and limit our potential and can become a source of contentiousness among people who think otherwise. Paul helps us to see that even in our profoundest moments we function within obvious limitations. "For now we see in a mirror dimly, but then face to face. Now I know in part; then shall I know fully, even as I have been fully known" (1 Corinthians 13:12). 1Corinthian 13 insists that we understand that love represents the only expression of the eternal that we bring into our ministry spaces. Our words and thoughts, while well-reasoned and researched, are filtered through "cracked pots" (2Corinthians 4:7a) and, at best, partial expressions of the truth. Such a sobering reality beckons us to lace our thoughts and opinions with a strong sense of humility of competence. The humbler we are about our own competence, the more the text opens to us and allows us to see and experience truths we don't know, or at least not considered.

Nonetheless, we are obligated to provide our listeners with opportunities to activate faith in concrete ways. The synthesis is the part in the sermon where we offer faith responses that are consistent with what has been declared in the proposition/thesis and described in the antithesis. The synthesis is the sentence that seeks to resolve the tension created by the first two sentences (the proposition and the antithesis). (Please refer to the Worksheet Exercise)

The synthesis is concerned primarily with answering the question that was raised within the Relevant Question.

The synthesis should answer the relevant question in some kind of order that makes it possible for the audience to follow." *–Proctor*

As the suggestive sentence, the synthesis suggests faith responses for the believers/hearers to consider as options to the anti-faith behavior stated in the antithesis.

The synthesis/suggestive provides some new-life perspectives for the believers/hearers to incorporate into their lives.

The suggestive/synthesis is the "what-to-do" part of the sermon.

The synthesis/suggestive statement draws from the biblical text some concrete faith responses, or new-life points to consider.

The synthesis/suggestive statement/sentence delivers the good news, or the hopefulness of the sermon.

The synthesis/suggestive statement provides the preacher with some clarity about the direction of the balance of the sermon.

The synthesis/suggestive sentence also provides the believers/hearers with a general outline by which the sermon can be remembered.

The synthesis/suggestive statement presents to the believers/hearers some concrete ways by which to consider afresh the relevancy of the Bible.

The synthesis/suggestive statement furthers the claims that Christian preaching really does matter!

SUGGESTED STEPS TO THE SYNTHESIS

1. Make certain you are clear about answering the relevant question in a logical and sensible manner.

2. Unless you are preaching a topical sermon, always mine the biblical text for the suggestions you want the audience to consider.

3. Always consider the action words of the text. What was important for the original hearers to do?

4. It is also helpful to consider the descriptive words of the text. How/why was it being described as such to the original hearers?

5. Work to condense your suggestions to three, no more than four sub-points. **NOTE**: It can be done with one!

6. Consider ways to make the suggestions memorable through creative mnemonic devices. For example, use alliterations, acrostics, or words/phrases beginning with same letter or same sound.

7. Always condense your answer to the relevant question into one powerfully suggestive sentence.

    Example: When we truly love God, we are moved to serve, sacrifice, and celebrate.

WHAT TO AVOID

1. Avoid disconnecting your suggestive statement from your relevant question.

2. Avoid disconnecting your suggestions from the interrogative specifics of your relevant question.

    Example: Don't answer "where?" or "what?" when you asked "how?"

3. Avoid disconnecting your suggestions from the biblical text.

4. Avoid running all over the Bible. Everything you need for the sermon is in the text before you!

5. Avoid disconnecting your suggestions from the issues raised in the descriptive/antithesis.

6. Avoid introducing matters disconnected from the biblical text.

AN EXAMPLE OF THE SYNTHESIS(SUGGESTIVE)

TEXT: Matthew 25:14-30

PROPOSITION: To make a meaningful contribution to life and living we must resist the religion of uselessness.

TITLE: "*The Religion of Uselessness*"

ANTITHESIS: We will never make meaningful contributions to life and living if we give in to the religion of uselessness.

THE RELEVANT QUESTION: How do we resist the religion of uselessness?

SYNTHESIS: We resist the religion of uselessness when we:

1. Understand ourselves as servants entrusted with something valuable (vss. 14-15);

2. Understand that using what we have beats hiding it any day (vss. 16-19);

3. Understand that there is no acceptable excuse for not using what we have (vss. 24-27).

A WORKSHEET EXERCISE ON THE SYNTHESIS

Continue the process of structuring the sermons used in the previous Worksheet Exercises and now include the synthesis. Again, utilize the "Steps To" and pay attention to "What to Avoid". The example provided on the previous page should be helpful.

TEXT: Psalm 23:1

PROPOSITION/THESIS: _____

_____

TITLE: _____

ANTITHESIS: _____

_____

SYNTHESIS: _____

1. _____

2. _____

3. _____

TEXT: Acts 8:1

PROPOSITION/THESIS: _____

_____

TITLE: _____

ANTITHESIS: _____

_____

SYNTHESIS: _____

1. _____

2. _____

3. _____

TEXT: John 2:5

PROPOSITION/THESIS: _____

_____

TITLE: _____

ANTITHESIS: _____

_____

SYNTHESIS: _____

1. _____

2. _____

3. _____

TEXT: Mark 1:9-11

PROPOSITION/THESIS: _____

_____

TITLE: _____

ANTITHESIS: _____

_____

SYNTHESIS: _____

1. _____

2. _____

3. _____

SHAPING THE SERMON:

The Essential Elements of the Sermon

Dr. Proctor practiced and promoted the following sermonic outline:

SUBJECT _____

TEXT _____

INTRODUCTION (ANTITHESIS) _____

TRANSITION (PROPOSITION/THESIS) _____

RELEVANT QUESTION_____

SYNTHESIS _____

1. _____

2. _____

3. _____

However, he also suggested utilizing a variety of approaches to avoid becoming predictable. I offer my understanding of the essential elements of the sermon below and see Appendix E for additional Worksheet Spaces.

THE INTRODUCTION

The introduction is the beginning of a sermon, in which the sermon's "main idea" is introduced.

RESOURCES FOR GOOD INTRODUCTIONS

- **Lived experiences**
- **Personal** – some personal experience, avoid TMI (Too Much Information!)
- **Observation** – something observed in your life, or in the life of another; autobiographies are rich resources for introductions.
- **Historical** – something factual and interesting from history.
- **Flip-It** – starting with the opposite of the main idea.
- **Not too serious** – start with something light.
- **Re-creation** – an imaginative re-creation of the text.
- **Current issue** – start with some current issue that demands a faith response.
- **Re-narrating a current event** – start with a current event that implicates the "main idea."
- **Fictional narrative** – start with a fictional story.
- **Cultural artifact** – start with a song, a poem, or some community commodity that connects with the sermon's idea and or antithesis.

THE BODY OF THE SERMON

The body of the sermon consists of the middle portion of the sermon, that which comes after the introduction and before the conclusion.

Within the body, we work out the details of the Thesis/Declarative and Antithesis/Descriptive, raise the Relevant Question/Interrogative, and create the Synthesis/Suggestive.

The Conclusion of the Sermon

The conclusion transitions to the end of the sermon.

The conclusion signals to the hearers that the proclaimed part of the sermon is coming to an end, and the living part of the sermon is about to begin.

SOME COMMON GOALS OF THE CONCLUSION

1. It opens a space for the listeners to respond to the sermon in some specific ways.

2. It summarizes the points stated in the Suggested.

3. It opens space to exhort the hearers to a higher calling.

4. It provides an illustration with a resolving image that rehearses the core or final thought of the sermon.

5. It provides the final resolution to narrative tension of the sermon.

6. Conclusions must conclude!

THE CELEBRATION

The celebration constitutes the peak moment of emotional, cognitive, and spiritual release.

The celebration is a unique experience in Black preaching that serves as an intensely emotional experience when the deepest aspects of the sermon are celebrated.

The celebration offers a unique opportunity to etch the sermon into the souls and psyche of the people.

REFERENCES FOR CELEBRATIONS

Dr. Frank Thomas provides an incredible treatment of celebration in his book, *They Like to Never Quit Praisin' God!*

Dr. Cleophus Larue probes the possibilities of celebration in Black preaching in his book, *Rethinking Celebration: From Rhetoric to Praise in African American Preaching.*

ON GETTING READY TO PREACH

"Lining Out the Sermon

Having a template, or sermon model matters. The homiletical model that a preacher uses helps in the perceiving, processing, preparing, packaging, and presenting of sermon ideas that matter. My wife's late mother, Earnestine Johnson Becton, was known to meticulously set out the necessary ingredients to be used in her amazing cooking exploits. At least a day ahead of the actual cooking, she would mix the seasonings. Specific cooking products would be set aside, and the primary ingredients of her cooking were purchased and secured. When asked about the wisdom of her detailed preparation, she responded, "I'm lining myself out." Diana, my beloved wife, who is an amazing cook in her own right, faithfully utilizes her mother's approach of "lining" herself out.

To be saved from the erratic and poor productions of the anxiety-filled "Saturday Night Special," the preacher needs a lining out approach. Like a well-prepared meal, whatever homiletical approach the preacher uses, she/he lines herself/himself out to prepare a sermon worthy of public consumption. Inherent to the Dialectical Model is a homiletical approach that effectively assists in the perceiving, processing, preparing, packaging, and presenting of sermon ideas. The Dialectical Model, as taught by Dr. Proctor, assists the preacher in lining out the sermon. Again:

The **Proposition** perceives an idea for which the preacher wrestles like Jacob wrestling with God, or him/herself.

The **Antithesis** helps to process the idea and determines whether it is worthy of proclamation.

The **Relevant Question** probes the relevancy of the sermonic idea for such a time as this.

The **Synthesis** packages the sermonic idea into usable increments for faith deployment. After such diligent lining out the preacher comes forth confident enough to present a sermon that matters.

As suggested above, I recommend developing a weekly practice of "lining out" one's sermon.

On Monday – rest, allow the mind to reset. Let the exhausted emotions be restored and the body to be healed from the sermonic exertions of Sunday. Every Sunday depletes something in the preacher that must be recovered.

On Tuesday – prepare the Proposition.

On Wednesday – prepare the Antithesis.

On Thursday – prepare the Relevant Question and Synthesis.

On Friday – write out the sermon following the suggested structure below.

On Saturday – pause, then polish the sermon, remove what's unnecessary, insert what's helpful.

On Sunday – preach as if your preaching matters because it does!

May each day be seasoned with prayerful intent.

THE DIALECTICAL MODEL IN A PANDEMIC STRICKEN WORLD:

Preaching Didactically

The once-in-a-lifetime Pandemic of COVID19 experience exposed a lot, but also taught us much. One of the things exposed was that much of what we were doing within worship, inclusive of the preaching moment was neither necessary nor essential. As a result, we were forced to condense our worship and modify our preaching. Our worship was condensed to the essentials of music, prayer and preaching. Coming out of the Pandemic, we now sing fewer songs, offer shorter prayers, and expedite giving by offering multiple giving platforms, i.e., Givlifly, CashApp, Zelle, etc..

Many of us modified our preaching on two fronts: We shortened the preaching time and added didactic features, with the hope of making our sermons more accessible. Secondly, with the use of PowerPoint, or Google slides we were able to share the main ideas of our sermons and hopefully impart life-giving lessons/truths.

I believe the Dialectical Model offers an excellent opportunity to be didactic and is incredibly helpful in accommodating the yet Pandemic affected church.

Here are a few suggestions on what I've done toward using the dialectical model in a didactic method.

From the written manuscript, prepare a slide to present Text, Topic, and a Key Word. In a recent sermon for Mother's Day, I presented on the screen the following:

Text: Proverbs 31:27

Topic: Making Momma Proud

WORD FOR THE DAY – Sacrifice (I use this word to identify the primary act of mothers, particularly mothers of marginalized children is to sacrifice.)

Share the Main Point. Using the just mentioned sermon, I posted on the screen the following:

MAIN POINT: Whenever children's lives are lived on an ascending trajectory, Mommas are made proud.

I do not necessarily present the antithesis on the monitors, but I will project images on the screen to illustrate it. However, I do prepare slides for each point provided in the synthesis, with relevant images.

For this sermon I used an acrostic to support the synthesis.

SYNTHESIS: If you want to make Momma proud use **M.A.P.S.** I explained that **M.A.P.S.** is an acrostic, a memory device to suggest that Momma is made proud when her children acknowledge and appreciate the sacrifices made to give them an opportunity to "rise up" in:

Mind – elevate one's mental capacities.

Image provided – graduation ceremonies.

Agency- elevate one's abilities to survive on one's own.

Image provided – young professionals.

People – elevate one's standing among the People (community).

Image provided – people active in community, serving in various capacities.

Soul – elevate one's spiritual capacity by cultivating one's soul.

Image provided – a baptismal experience. (We baptized that day, and I used the young man baptized as a living example of M.A.P.S.)

When preparing a didactic sermon, I suggest the following:

1. **Use Simple Language:** Use simple and concise language that the listeners can understand. Avoid using complex terminology or technical jargon that may only confuse people. Simple language includes simple sentences.

2. **Connect with the Audience**: A sermon best connects with the audience when it focuses on the listeners' needs. Use examples, analogies, or personal stories that resonate with them or relate the message to current events and concerns.

3. **Structure the Sermon**: Have a clear and logical structure to the sermon. Follow a clear outline that includes an introduction, body, and conclusion. Use transitions that smoothly move the listener from one point to the next. (See the above section on Structure Matters.)

4. **Use Visual Aids:** Use visual aids, such as PowerPoint slides, Google Slides, or videos to illustrate key points and make the message more engaging. Visual aids also assist in capturing and holding people's attention. During an Annual gathering of the Full Gospel Baptist Church Fellowship, I witnessed Presiding Bishop Joseph W. Walker, III use a video loop of a flying eagle as an illustration. The image of the flying eagle riveted in our minds the point of God's desire for us to soar.

5. **Ask Questions**: Encourage participation and understanding by asking questions. Using a method borrowed from my dear friend and preacher par excellent, Dr. Edward L. Branch, I open with a probing question. It's important to pause and allow listeners a moment to consider the questions and reflect on their meaning for the message.

6. **Provide Takeaways:** Give the listeners practical steps they can take to apply the message in their daily lives. Provide scripts and direction on how they can use the principles to better their lives. In the above sermon, the takeaway was **M.A.P.S. M.A.P.S.** provided a literal life map to assist in making Momma proud.

7. **Make it Memorable:** The late C.A.W. Clark once described "a great sermon is one the people remember." Use memorable stories, quotes, and illustrations to reinforce the key points of the message. It encourages retention of the message. Dr. Frederick Douglas Haynes, III, is an excellent user of personal and memorable stories in preaching. Dr. Harry S. Wright, former president of Bishop College, and retired Pastor of Cornerstone Baptist Church, Brooklyn, NY, set a standard for storytelling in preaching. The late Dr. T. M. Chambers of Los Angeles had a practice of repeating each sentence of his sermons at least three times. His repetitiveness was brilliantly modulated and never became a source of irritation.

8. **Point out God in it All**: It is essential that we encourage listeners to find God in all aspects of their lives by unifying all topics to the gospel message. Be certain to tie the message back to Jesus's teachings and encourage people to reflect and act accordingly.

Dr. Proctor was a superb storyteller, but he told stories to help people grow closer to God, and to build personal agency and community by imparting knowledge and a deeper understanding of the Biblical texts. By using clear language, relevant examples, and practical takeaways, he employed the Dialectical Model to didactically make the sermon more accessible and, thus, allowed more people to connect more deeply to the gospel message.

SERMONS AS LIVING ORGANISMS

Resurrection Empowered Preaching

Sermons are living organisms. If sermons are to give life, they must have life. Dead sermons perpetuate death, and rank with the stench of the preacher's dead approach to preaching. I contend that the Resurrection of Jesus provides preaching with the theological impetus to declare new life in a world shrouded in death. We who preach from the energy source of the Resurrection preach life, and we do so most often in places and spaces of death. Because the Resurrection is a declaration of life, sermons represent living organisms and are designed to perpetuate life. A Resurrection minded sermon is critical to preaching a sermon that matters.

I grew up listening to preachers who ended every sermon, no matter the text, celebrating, "He died, but early Sunday morning He got up!" This was such a common part of the Black preaching experience that many of my early preaching mentors believed and taught that preaching was incomplete without journeying by the Cross and the empty tomb. Perhaps such preaching was necessary to them because of the ubiquitous death-dealing realities of Black life in America. Black enslavement was death and the Jim Crow South, and its Northern, Midwestern, and Western residuals eventuated more death. Emphasizing the Resurrection gave hope to broken Blacks whose lives were surrounded with so much death.

However, I later learned and discovered that not every sermon neither demanded, accommodated, or required a celebrative trip by Calvary and an announcement of the empty tomb. Moreover, I deduced that Jesus didn't die. He was murdered. According to James Cone, like thousands of Black people, he was lynched![31] Neither did he get up, or he didn't get up on his own power. The testimony of the Bible is that God raised Jesus from the dead (Romans 6:10-11). Consequently, my early preaching experiences struggled with connecting the Resurrection with every sermon I preached. I struggled until one day God did for my theology and hermeneutics what God did for Jesus. God theologically and hermeneutically raised me up!

After years of struggling to theologically construct a resurrection perspective beyond the popular sermonic claim of "He got up!" a switch came on. It occurred to me that the **Resurrection powerfully proclaims God's surprise of new life where death ought to be.** Regardless of how one looks at the Resurrection, whether literally or metaphorically, resurrection is about the discovery of new life in places designed for death. Such an understanding seems to have informed the preaching of Paul when he wrote, "That I may know him and the power of his Resurrection, and may share his sufferings, becoming like him in his death, that by any means possible I may attain the resurrection from the dead" (Philippians 3:10-11, NIV).

Because Jesus lives, sermons about him ought to live! The Resurrection testifies of God's insistence on providing life, especially within contexts threatened by death. Thus, the Resurrection fuels the preaching experience with the impetus to bring new life in places of death. Ezekiel demonstrated preaching as an experience of resurrection when he was called upon by God to preach to a valley of dry bones (Ezekiel 37). We, too, are called upon to infuse our preaching with resurrection power and intent.

---

31 James Cone, The Cross and the Lynching Tree. Orbis Books: Maryknoll, NY, 2011.

Admittedly, like Dr. Proctor, my life-long search for truth and understanding has prompted me to re-think, and in some instances discard much of the theological assumptions of my upbringing. I learned that much of what was being espoused as essential Christian doctrines were theological constructs designed to advance the deadly idolatries of white male privilege. However, I retain a dogged belief in the Resurrection as the definitive experience of the Christian faith. Such a belief shapes what I understand about preaching, as well as what I preach. Like Paul, I yearn to "know him and the power of his Resurrection." Hence, my commitment to resurrection minded preaching.

Resurrection-minded preaching is a powerful and transformative approach to preaching that focuses on the redemptive power of Christ's resurrection. It emphasizes that the good news of the gospel is not just about forgiveness of sin and an escape from eternal damnation but also about the hope and new life that come through the resurrection of Jesus Christ. Resurrection-minded preaching acknowledges the suffering and the brokenness in the world but proclaims that through the resurrection, Christ has overcome death and has the power to bring new life to all who believe in him. This approach to preaching provides a message of hope, encourages spiritual transformation, and helps believers to live out the reality of Christ's resurrection in their daily lives.

Resurrection minded preaching views preaching as a resurrection experience in several ways, as demonstrated by various biblical examples:

1. **Resurrection minded preaching brings dead words to life** - In Ezekiel 37, the prophet recounts his vision of a valley of dry bones, which represent the people of Israel who have lost their hope and are spiritually dead. But, as God commands, Ezekiel prophesies over the bones, and they come to life, becoming a mighty army. Preaching has the power to bring dead words and spirits to life by delivering a message of hope and faith.

2. **Resurrection minded preaching restores spiritual sight** - In John 9, Jesus heals a man who was born blind. During the healing process, Jesus asks the man to wash in the Pool of Siloam, and the man's sight is restored. The man then goes and testifies to the people and the self-righteous religionists about his healing, which provides an opportunity for Jesus to preach the truth about his mission and divine power. Preaching has the power to open blind eyes and restore spiritual sight while revealing the truth of Christ's redemptive work. I took a month working on this text around the idea, "The Power of a New Story." **PROPOSITION: We need a Jesus moment that allows us to see that the most powerful thing that can happen in the life of a person, a church, a people, or a country is to embrace the new life possibilities of a new story.**

3. **Resurrection minded preaching speaks truth to power** - In Acts 24, Paul is brought before the governor, Felix, who is skeptical about Paul's message. Despite this, Paul boldly preaches the truth about Christ and the gospel, even though it could mean his own death. Preaching has the power to speak truth to power, even in the face of persecution or opposition.

4. **Resurrection minded preaching transforms hearts** - In Acts 2, Peter preaches a powerful sermon on the Day of Pentecost, and the Holy Spirit falls upon the people, causing a radical transformation in their hearts. They repent of their sins, are baptized, and become part of the early Christian community.

Preaching has the power to transform hearts and minds by convicting people of sin and leading them to repentance and salvation.

In all the above examples, preaching represents a resurrection experience by bringing new life, restoring sight, speaking truth, and transforming hearts. Through resurrection minded preaching, the good news of the gospel is proclaimed, and people are brought into the light of Christ's resurrection, experiencing the power of renewed life and transformation.

I further emphasize that the dialectical model as taught by Samuel Dewitt Proctor literally raises preaching from the dead and gives it new life. The dialectical essentials facilitate resurrection-minded preaching.

A WORKBOOK EXERCISE

1. How has the Resurrection shaped your understanding of preaching?

_____

_____

_____

_____

_____

_____

2. In what ways do you incorporate the Resurrection in your preaching?

_____

_____

_____

_____

_____

_____

APPENDIX A

HOMILETICAL WORDS
"CONSTRUCTION"

Con - "with"

+

Structure - "related form"

= Construction

EXEGESIS
"To lead out"

The exegesis is the responsible process by which one examines the biblical text with a view toward determining the original intention of the text.

Dialectical

The dialectical approach is constructed around a method of logic that uses an obvious truth and its relationship to an exposed falsehood in order to offer a preferred response.

APPENDIX B

BIBLICAL DEFINITIONS OF PREACHING

The following words represent the various ways in which "preaching" is used in the New Testament:

KERRUSO

To preach in the New Testament is "to proclaim as a herald." The word used is "kerruso."

KERRUSSO

Kerrusso was a public activity used to convey what the early believers believed was an approach to life that mattered.

EUANGELLIZZO

Euangellizo means *"to preach,"* to tell the good news. This word describes both the method and the message:

- preaching (telling) is the method
- the "good news" is the message.

This word is used about seventy times in the New Testament, including Matthew 11:5, Luke 3:18, and Acts 5:42.

LALEO

Laleo means "to talk," "to converse," "to tell." Literally, it means "to talk it up." It gives the idea of the more personal approach suggested by a conversation.

In your Bible, this word is usually translated "to speak" or "to talk." It is used more than 250 times in the New Testament. Acts 11:19 illustrates this method well.

MARTUREO

Martureo means "to be a witness" or "to testify." This word gives the idea of a convincing testimony based on genuine convictions and clear evidence.

This method of communicating the gospel is used more than seventy times in the New Testament. John 1:7–8, 15; Acts 1:8; 5:32; and 14:3 are examples of this method.

DIALEGOMAI

Dialegomai means "to hold dialogue." This word suggests an exchange of views, an opportunity to question and interact on the message presented. It is the opposite of monologue, in which the speaking is done by one person. Here a teaching-learning situation exists. It occurs a few times in the New Testament; the following are examples of this method: Mark 9:35; Acts 17:2, 17; 18:4.

KATANGELLO

Katangello means "to tell thoroughly and with authority." Two other words, *plero* and *parresiazomai*, add to the idea of thoroughness and authority with respective meanings of "to fill" and "to speak openly, boldly." References for this word are found in Acts 13:38; 15:36; and 17:3.

Consider the different terms used for preaching in the following text:

> *The Spirit of the Lord is on me, because he has anointed me to preach good news [euangellizo] to the poor. He has sent me to proclaim [kerusso] freedom for the prisoners and recovery of sight for the blind, to release the oppressed, to proclaim [kerusso] the year of the Lord's favor.* –Luke 4:18–19

APPENDIX C

JUICING THE SERMON

The term "juicing the sermon" suggests interjecting the sermon with what I call image stimulants. Image stimulants do exactly as implied—provide images that stimulate. Well-crafted words embedded within the sermon stimulate the sermon with sensory perceptions that increase the sermon's life-giving purposes.

Life-filled words invigorate the sensory possibilities of the sermon, thereby providing greater access to the hearers' minds. In this overly stimulated world, the preacher needs to be mindful of the following:

Sermons need **images** to project truth upon the screens of people's minds.

Sermons need sense **provocations** to impress upon the sensitivities of people.

Sermons need **insights** to equip a faith response to hope-killing realities.

Sermons need **instructions** to allow people opportunities to live life differently.

APPENDIX D

PREACHING EULOGIES THAT MATTER

A THEOLOGY OF DEATH FOR EULOGIES

THE WITNESS CIRCLE

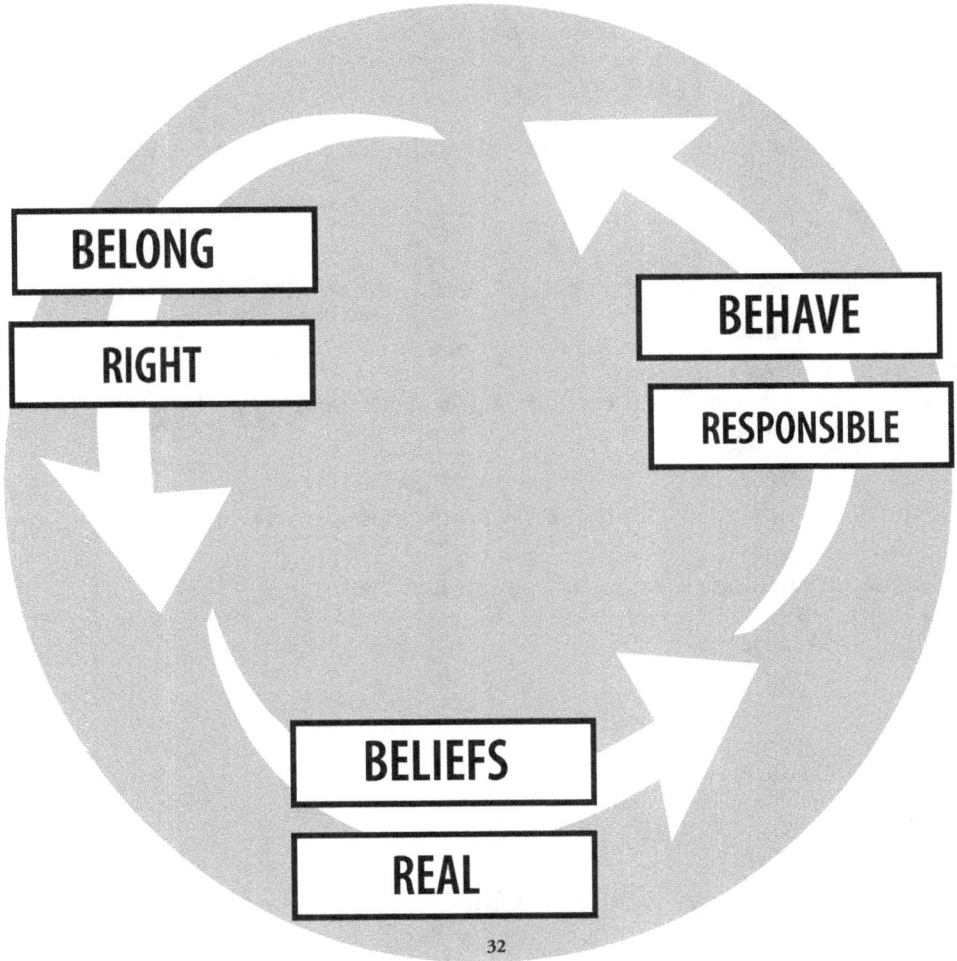

BELONG

RIGHT

BEHAVE

RESPONSIBLE

BELIEFS

REAL

32

The above self-assessment tool allows us to examine the veracity of our belief systems. While the arrows within the circle interact, we often begin with **BELIEFS**. The argument portends that what we believe shows up in our **BEHAVIOR**. Consequently, how we behave impacts the quality of how we **BELONG**. The challenge is to make sure that what we believe is **REAL**, how we behave is **RESPONSIBLE**, and how

---

32   The Witness Circle was developed during the Practicum of a Master's Degree in Mental Health and Counseling at the California Institute of Integrated Studies, San Francisco, California, 2012. I have since used it in a variety of ways in teaching and ministry.

we belong is **RIGHT**. Right in this instance is interacting with one another in ways that are just, and not intrusive, abusive, or imposing.

If one's BELIEFS are not real, they lead to BEHAVIOR that is not responsible. Likewise, if our BEHAVIOR is not responsible it creates BELONGING that is not right. An assessment demands that we either reexamine our BELIEFS or realign irresponsible BEHAVIOR to the reality of our BELIEFS.

If our BEHAVIOR corrupts how we BELONG, we must readjust our BEHAVIOR or reconsider our BELONGING. It should be noted that BELIEFS are often products of where we BELONG, and communal/BELONG-based beliefs are no guarantee of right/real BELIEFS.

The interconnectedness of the BELIEFS, BEHAVIOR, AND BELONG give us an opportunity to self-correct on several levels.

In matters of ministry, we can never do well practically what we have not wrestled with theologically.

Preaching constitutes a theological act.

As a theological act, when we preach, we make public our theological understandings, and oftentimes our theological misunderstandings.

Samuel Dewitt Proctor noted, "In preaching, a preacher's theology is exposed." –(Proctor, *The Certain Sound of The Trumpet*)

Nowhere is the depth of a preacher's theology more exposed than when presenting eulogies.

It could be argued that eulogies represent a time when a sermon is

- most needed
- most heard
- most remembered
- most transformative.

A classical definition of theology is Saint Anselm's "faith seeking understanding."

Preaching eulogies demands that we seriously ponder the following:

What is it we understand/believe about death?

Where did those understandings/beliefs come from?

How well have those understandings/beliefs served us?

Do those understandings/beliefs provide us with a belief perspective that enables us to live beyond the experience of death?

And are those understandings/beliefs valid enough to shape a testimony worthy of sharing with someone else?

The experience and reality of death force people to a moment when their faith seeks understanding.

Classical theology generally draws from four major sources:

- Scripture

- Reasoning

- Tradition

- Experience

Black Theology adds to the theological query:

Black Culture

Black history

To shape a theology of death we, too, must draw from the reliable sources that have served the church well through the ages:

- **Scripture** – Death is viewed openly (Psalm 23:4); Death is embraced (Genesis 50:24); Death is celebrated (1Corinthians 15:50ff); Death is utilized (Deuteronomy 13:5); Death is villainized (1Corinthians 15:26); Death is overcome (1Corinthians 15:55)

- **Reasoning** – Death has been explored, prayed over, and reflected upon by the most informed thinkers in history and in the life of the Church. Clearly death has been perceived as an inevitable part of the human experience: everyone who has ever lived has died from one thing or another.

- **Tradition** – Our traditions reveal that death has been respected, examined, wrestled with, denied, accepted, exploited, feared, and celebrated across the years within the Christian church. A responsible theologian invites and welcomes the voices of believers across the centuries.

- **Experience-** Death as an inevitable dimension of the human experience has been subjected to the scrutiny of the biblical text and viewed realistically, not fatalistically, fictitiously, or avoidantly.

In Black theology, all traditional sources of theology are re-thought through the lenses of the Black experience. Black theology critiques the many racist and bigoted assumptions of Western theology.

In Black theology oppressive constructs and ideologies embedded within Western theology are critiqued, condemned, and reformatted to address the Black experience.

Because of such obvious and pervasive oppression, where Black life is either demonized, minimized, marginalized, or "invisibilized," Black Theology adds

Black History – Black history consists of the lived experiences of Black people in a context often defined by the ominous threat of death. Death is re-imagined and embraced with the hopefulness of:

- Ancestral witness – the deceased living among us (Hebrews 12:1)

- A state of being – being alive versus living (Dante Quick)[33]

- Empowerment – releasing one's spirit to the divine – Luke 23:46

- Ultimate victory over oppressive realities --1Corinthians 15:55-57)

Black Culture – Black Culture embraces the distinct artifacts that the Black community has created to give expression to its life, beliefs, behavior, and ways of belonging.

Black people's creations around death have almost always had to do with being delivered from the painful realities of black life in America. Some of those cultural artifacts are:

- Makeshift altars

- "Pouring one out"- a libation of an alcoholic beverage*

- "Lighting one up"- the lighting up of a marijuana cigarette*

- Placing of gloves – tossing flowers

- "Cooling boards and winding sheets"

- Sitting with the bereaved

- Cooking for the bereaved

*(While these expressions are not always encouraged, or universally embraced, preachers do well to acknowledge their practice and what it means for the mourners.)

EXAMPLES OF CULTURAL ARTIFACTS IN SONG AND PROSE

"One of these mornings,
Won't be very long.
You'll look for me,
And, I'll be gone. (Psalm 55:4-6)

"I want to die easy when I die.
I want to die easy when I die.
Shout salvation as I fly,
I want to die easy as I die."
(Howard Thurman, *The Negro Spiritual Speaks of Life and Death*)

---

33 Dr. Dante Quick, PhD served as Professor of Preaching and Ethics for the Bay Area Academy of Responsible Preaching of Leadership Institute at Allen Temple, Oakland, CA.

PREACHING EULOGIES THAT LIVE

"Blessed are those who mourn, for they will be comforted. (Matthew 5:4, NRSV)"

Preaching funerals demand sensitivity to the experience of loss. Death represents not just the loss of a loved one, but the loss of

- a way of life;

- a meaningful relationship;

- personal and family perspective,

- community representative.

No context exposes the frailty of human life like a funeral.

"All go to one place. All are from the dust, and to dust all return. (Ecclesiastes 3:20, NIV)"

In the Black church were the body is often present, people are brought face-to-face with the inevitability of death.

"A time to be born, and a time to die. (Ecclesiastes 3:3, NIV).

The sermon preached at a funeral is called a "eulogy."

Eu – "good"

Logos – "words"

A eulogy means to "**speak well**" of someone who has died.

NOTE: *Speaking well* does not mean the preacher stretches the truth, fabricates or speaks falsely.

"In order for some people to look good, people expect the preacher to start hallucinating ." Reverend Al Sharpton

As a caring pastor and thoughtful student of preaching, I developed the following approach to eulogies from studying the Reverend Dr. Amos Jones, Jr.. As a Divinity student at Vanderbilt and member of the Westwood Baptist Church, University Center, Nashville, I witnessed and took note of his brilliant and masterful approach to eulogies. He was consistently good. While he never shared with me what he was doing, or instructed me how to do a eulogy, this is my interpretation and reframing of what I perceived him to do. In alliterative summary, for eulogies I seek to do the following:

- **DIGNIFY THE DECEASED**

- **EDIFY THE BEREAVED**

- **GLORIFY GOD**

DIGNIFYING THE DECEASED

We can dignify the deceased by:

- Concentrating on the **good** he or she brought into the world;

- personalizing the eulogy by lifting up positive **character** traits, **unique gifts/talents**, personality idiosyncrasies;

- acknowledging how he or she was **loved.**

SOURCES FOR DIGNIFYING THE DECEASED

- Personal knowledge and interactions – reflect!

- Interactions and experiences of family and friends – ask!

- Consult the Obituary – read!

- Listen to the "Words of Comfort" shared in the funeral – listen!

EDIFYING THE BEREAVED

We can edify the bereaved by:

- Lifting up the relational dynamics and citing the love shared;

- helping the bereaved celebrate life in the face of death;

- offering words of hope and comfort;

- intentionally make the deceased and the bereaved the most important people in the space.

SOURCES FOR EDIFYING THE BEREAVED

- Personal knowledge and experiences – reflect!

- Inquiring of family and friends – inquire!

- Listen to the "Words of Comfort" shared in the funeral – listen!

GLORIFYING GOD

- Acknowledge God as the giver and sustainer of life.

- Rejoice in the love of God – "neither death shall separate us from the love of God."

- Celebrate the comfort and hope God provides.

THE BIBLE IN THE FUNERAL

- Anchor the eulogy in the Bible;

- locate stories and/or texts that accentuates the deceased's life and/witness;

- weave the Bible's witness into the witness of the deceased, or the hope of the bereaved;

- celebrate the Christian victory!

THE DIALECTICAL MODEL AND THE EULOGY

The dialectical model can be used in a sermon in the following manner:

- Develop a proposition;

- Shape a soft antithesis – minimize the tension;

- Shape a Narrative Sermon – the sermon is about the story of life, not the experience of death;

- As is reasonably possible, always conclude celebrating the Christian hope - Resurrection/Eschatology!

THE PREACHER'S PERSONHOOD IN A FUNERAL

The Preacher's personal capacity to facilitate the funeral is vital. Be honest about your own strengths and acknowledge your weaknesses. How the preacher shows up matters!

The loss of a loved one stirs deep emotions, and the likelihood of family challenges and disruptions are great. Separate your own issues from what a family might be experiencing and meet them where they are.

People have been known to use death as an opportunity to settle unresolved family conflicts. (Never referee family conflict before a funeral, and certainly not during the eulogy!)

Avoid pimping grief! I risk using provocative language with the hope of bringing some consideration to the oft used practice of using funeral to evangelize. I am clear that death possesses the potential to prompt people to do things differently in their lives, but I find it poor taste to exploit moments of personal loss to grow the church. Jesus said, "And I, if I be lifted up from the earth, I'll draw all persons unto me. (John 12:32)" Let Jesus do what Jesus does best and let us do what we can best do in that moment – preach a eulogy that matters!

Consider The Psalm 23 Model on the next page as a few tips on the pastoral disposition of the Preacher's Personhood in a Funeral.

THE PREACHER'S PERSONHOOD IN A FUNERAL – The Psalm 23 Model

The Preacher's capacity to facilitate the funeral is vital. The loss of a loved one stirs deep emotions, and the likelihood of family challenges and disruptions is great.

As a representative of the Good Shepherd, the preacher should display:

Presence – Psalm 23:1-2a

Direction – Psalm 23:2b

Strength – Psalm 23:3

Comfort – Psalm 23:4

Protection – Psalm 23:5

Hopefulness – Psalm 23:6

AN EXAMPLE OF RECENTLY PREACHED EULOGY – I consider this a "Character Sermon," although no one knows anything about the character mentioned in the biblical text. I use the character's anonymity to connect with the less known character of the deceased.

TEXT: "*Thomas, who was called the Twin, said to his fellow disciples, "Let us also go, that we may die with him."* (John 11:16, NRSV)

TOPIC: A Witness for Wally Stuart: Jimmy's Brother

OPENING PARAGRAPH: One of the most important lessons we can learn within the context of family is how to celebrate the life and worth of a sibling whose life is eclipsed by another sibling.

OPENING STORY: The call I received from Jimmy's wife informing me of the death of Jimmy's brother, a brother who I knew nothing about. When I reached out to Jimmy, he uncharacteristically shared details with me of his brother's life.

PROPOSITION: "Jimmy's Brother" is about God gifting us with people whose lives are most often lived in obscurity, but without whom we would never be who we are.

BIBLICAL TEXT: I note the unknown, unmentioned, un-cited, non-detectable twin.

CONSIDER JIMMY: An amazing, well-known, well-thought of brother, a pillar of the church.

CONSIDER JIMMY'S BROTHER: He was not as well-known. In fact, many within the current congregation didn't know him.

RELEVANT QUESTION: How do we celebrate a brother who was largely absent, not well-known, (not known by many, including me)?

SYNTHESIS: We give a witness for Jimmy's brother because:

1. He gives us an opportunity to love unconditionally.

2. He gives us an opportunity to see in him what God sees in us.

3. He gives us an opportunity to celebrate inclusion and diversity.

APPENDIX E

PREACHING WORKSHEET SPACES

TEXT: _____

PROPOSITION (Declarative Statement):

_____

_____

_____

_____

TITLE: _____

ANTITHESIS (Descriptive Statement):

_____

_____

_____

_____

_____

RELEVANT QUESTION (Interrogative Statement):

_____

_____

_____

SYNTHESIS (Suggestive Statement):

1. _____

2. _____

3. _____

TEXT: _____

PROPOSITION (Declarative Statement):

_____

_____

_____

_____

_____

TITLE: _____

ANTITHESIS (Descriptive Statement):

_____

_____

_____

_____

_____

RELEVANT QUESTION (Interrogative Statement):

_____

_____

_____

SYNTHESIS (Suggestive Statement):

1. _____

2. _____

3. _____

TEXT: _____

PROPOSITION (Declarative Statement):

_____

_____

_____

_____

_____

TITLE: _____

ANTITHESIS (Descriptive Statement):

_____

_____

_____

_____

_____

RELEVANT QUESTION (Interrogative Statement):

_____

_____

_____

SYNTHESIS (Suggestive Statement):

1. _____

2. _____

3. _____

TEXT: _____

PROPOSITION (Declarative Statement):

_____

_____

_____

_____

_____

TITLE: _____

ANTITHESIS (Descriptive Statement):

_____

_____

_____

_____

_____

RELEVANT QUESTION (Interrogative Statement):

_____

_____

_____

SYNTHESIS (Suggestive Statement):

1. _____

2. _____

3. _____

TEXT: _____

PROPOSITION (Declarative Statement):

_____

_____

_____

_____

_____

TITLE: _____

ANTITHESIS (Descriptive Statement):

_____

_____

_____

_____

_____

RELEVANT QUESTION (Interrogative Statement):

_____

_____

_____

SYNTHESIS (Suggestive Statement):

1. _____

2. _____

3. _____

TEXT: _____

PROPOSITION (Declarative Statement):

_____

_____

_____

_____

_____

TITLE: _____

ANTITHESIS (Descriptive Statement):

_____

_____

_____

_____

RELEVANT QUESTION (Interrogative Statement):

_____

_____

_____

SYNTHESIS (Suggestive Statement):

1. _____

2. _____

3. _____

A PRAYER FOR PREACHING

We thank You for the awesome privilege of being able to preach Your Word. We thank You that we do not have to create something new, but that we are blessed to employ Your Everlasting Word each week. We are thankful that as we study and as we preach, we have Your Divine Promise that Your Word will accomplish the intended purpose. Help us, Dear God to trust that promise, to trust that every Word of Scripture is true, perfect, and a blessing to everyone who hears it. May those of us who preach deliver Your Word, with love and grace. May we preach with passion and compassion. May our hearts be filled and overflowing with Your Word. In the Name of The Word who became flesh we pray, Amen. (Jenkins Institute, November 2022)

SELECTED BIBLIOGRAPHY

Reference Works

McClure, John S. *Preaching Words: 144 Key Terms in Homiletics*. Louisville: Westminster John Knox Press, 2007.

Simmons, Martha, and Frank A. Thomas. *Preaching With Sacred Fire: An Anthology of African American Preaching, 1750-Present*. New York: W.W. Norton, 2010.

Willimon, William H., and Richard Lischer. *Concise Encyclopedia of Preaching*. Louisville: Westminster John Knox Press, 1995.

Wilson, Paul Scott, ed. *The New Interpreter's Handbook of Preaching*. Nashville: Abingdon Press, 2008.

African American Preaching

Andrews, Dale P. *Practical Theology for Black Churches: Bridging Black Theology and African American Folk Religion*. Louisville: Westminster John Knox Press, 2002.

Blount, Brian K. *Go Preach! Mark's Kingdom Message and the Black Church Today*. Maryknoll, NY: Orbis Books, 1998.

Bond, L. Susan. *Contemporary African American Preaching: Diversity in Theory & Style*. St. Louis, MO: Chalice Press, 2003.

Cannon, Katie Geneva. *Teaching Preaching: Isaac Rufus Clark and Black Sacred Rhetoric*. New York: Continuum International Publishing Group, 2002.

Collier-Thomas, Bettye. *Daughters of Thunder: Black Women Preachers and Their Sermons, 1850-1979*. San Francisco: Jossey-Bass, 1997.

Crawford, Evans E., and Thomas H. Troeger. *The Hum: Call and Response in African American Preaching*. Nashville: Abingdon Press, 1995.

Davis, Gerald L. *I Got the Word in Me and I Can Sing It, You Know: A Study of the Performed African-American Sermon*. Philadelphia: University of Pennsylvania Press, 1985.

Forbes, James A. *The Holy Spirit and Preaching*. Nashville: Abingdon Press, 1989.

Fry Brown, Teresa L. *Weary Throats and New Songs: Black Women Proclaiming God's Word*. Nashville: Abingdon Press, 2003.

_____. *Delivering the Sermon: Voice, Body, and Animation in Proclamation*. Minneapolis: Fortress Press, 2008.

Gilbert, Kenyatta R. *The Journey and Promise of African American Preaching (Creative Pastoral Care and Counseling)*. Philadelphia: Fortress Press, 2011.

Harris, James Henry. *Preaching Liberation*. Minneapolis, MN: Fortress Press, 1995.

_____ *The Word Made Plain: The Power and Promise of Preaching*. Minneapolis: Fortress Press, 1995.

Haskins, James. *Keeping the Faith: African American Sermons of Liberation.* New York: Welcome Rain Publishers, 2002.

Hatcher, William E. *John Jasper: The Unmatched Negro Philosopher and Preacher.* Chapel Hill, NC: Academic Affairs Library, University of North Carolina at Chapel Hill, 2000.

Haywood, Chanta M. *Prophesying Daughters: Black Women Preachers and the Word, 1823- 1913.* Columbia, MO: University of Missouri Press, 2003.

Jackson, Ronald L. II, and Elaine B. Richardson, eds. *Understanding African American Rhetoric: Classical Origins to Contemporary Innovations.* New York: Routledge, 2003.

Jea, John B. *The Life, History, and Unparalleled Sufferings of John Jea, the African Preacher.* Chapel Hill, NC: Academic Affairs Library, University of North Carolina at Chapel Hill, 2001.

Johnson, James Weldon, Aaron Douglas, C. B. Falls. *God's Trombones Seven Negro Sermons in Verse.* Chapel Hill, NC: University of North Carolina at Chapel Hill Libraries, 2004.

Jones, Kirk Byron. *The Jazz of Preaching: How to Preach with Freedom and Joy.* Nashville: Abingdon Press, 2004.

LaRue, Cleophus J. *The Heart of Black Preaching.* Louisville: Westminster John Knox Press, 2000.

_____, ed. *Power in the Pulpit: How America's Most Effective Black Preachers Prepare Their Sermons.* Louisville: Westminster John Knox Press, 2002.

_____, ed. *More Power in the Pulpit: How America's Most Effective Black Preachers Prepare Their Sermons.* *1ˢᵗ Edition.* Louisville: Westminster John Knox Press, 2009.

_____. *I Believe I'll Testify: The Art of African American Preaching.* Louisville: Westminster John Knox Press, 2011.

Lassiter, Valentino. *Martin Luther King in the African American Preaching Tradition.* Cleveland, OH: Pilgrim Press, 2001.

Lischer, Richard. *The Preacher King: Martin Luther King, Jr. and the Word That Moved America.* New York: Oxford University Press, 1995.

Massey, James Earl. *Designing the Sermon: Order and Movement in Preaching.* Abingdon Preacher's Library. Nashville: Abingdon Press, 1980.

McMickle, Marvin Andrew. *Preaching to the Black Middle Class: Words of Challenge, Words of Hope.* Valley Forge, PA: Judson Press, 2000.

_____. *Shaping the Claim: Moving From Texts to Sermon (Elements of Preaching).* Minneapolis: Fortress Press, 2008.

Mitchell, Ella Pearson. *Those Preaching Women, Vols. 1and 2.* Valley Forge, PA: Judson Press, 1985.

_____. *Those Preaching Women, Vol. 3.* Valley Forge, PA: Judson Press, 1996.

Mitchell, Henry H. *The Recovery of Preaching.* San Francisco: Harper & Row Publishers, 1977.

_____. *Black Preaching: The Recovery of a Powerful Art.* Nashville: Abingdon Press, 1990.

_____. *Celebration and Experience in Preaching*. Nashville: Abingdon Press, 1990, rev. 2008.

Moyd, Olin P. *The Sacred Art: Preaching & Theology in the African American Tradition*. Valley Forge, PA: Judson Press, 1995.

Pipes, William H. *Say Amen, Brother! Old-Time Negro Preaching—A Study in American Frustration*. Detroit: Wayne State University Press, 1992.

Powery, Luke. *Spirit Speech: Celebration and Lament in Preaching*. Nashville: Abingdon Press, 2009.

Proctor, Samuel D. *"How Shall They Hear?" Effective Preaching for Vital Faith*. Valley Forge, PA: Judson Press, 1992.

_____. *The Certain Sound of the Trumpet: Crafting a Sermon of Authority*. Valley Forge, PA: Judson Press, 1994.

Randolph, Edwin Archer. *The Life of Rev. John Jasper, Pastor of Sixth Mt. Zion Baptist Church, Richmond, Va., From His Birth to the Present Time, with His Theory on the Rotation of the Sun*. Chapel Hill, NC: Academic Affairs Library, University of North Carolina at Chapel Hill, 2001.

Roberts, Samuel K., ed. *Born to Preach: Essays in Honor of the Ministry of Henry and Ella Mitchell*. Valley Forge, PA: Judson Press, 2000.

Rosenberg, Bruce A. *Can These Bones Live? The Art of the American Folk Preacher*. Urbana: University of Illinois Press, rev.1988.

Simmons, Martha, ed. *Preaching on the Brink: The Future of Homiletics*. Nashville: Abingdon Press, 1996.

Simmons, Martha, and Frank A. Thomas. *Preaching with Sacred Fire: An Anthology of African American Preaching, 1750 to the Present*. New York: W. W. Norton & Company, Inc., 2010.

Simmons, Martha J., and Frank A. Thomas. *9.11.01: African American Leaders Respond to an American Tragedy Nine Eleven Zero One*. Valley Forge, PA: Judson Press, 2001.

Smith, Kelly Miller. *Social Crisis Preaching*. Macon, GA: Mercer University Press, 1984.

Spencer, Jon Michael. *Sacred Symphony: The Chanted Sermon of the Black Preacher*. New York: Greenwood Press, 1987.

Stewart, Warren H. *Interpreting God's Word in Black Preaching*. Valley Forge, PA: Judson Press, 1984.

Taylor, Gardner C. *How Shall They Preach?* Elgin, IL: Progressive Baptist Publishing House, 1977.

Thomas, Frank A. *They Like to Never Quit Praisin' God: The Role of Celebration in Preaching*. Cleveland, OH: United Church Press, 1997.

Titon, Jeff Todd. *Give Me This Mountain: Life, History, and Selected Sermons of C. L. Franklin*. Urbana, IL: University of Illinois Press, 1989.

Turner, William Clair, Jr. *Preaching that Makes the Word Plain: Doing Theology in the Crucible of Life*. Eugene: OR: Cascade Books, 2008.

Warren, Mervyn A. *King Came Preaching: The Pulpit Power of Dr. Martin Luther King, Jr.* Downers Grove, IL: InterVarsity Press, 2001.

Asian Preaching

Kim, Eunjoo Mary. *Preaching the Presence of God: A Homiletic from an Asian American Perspective.* Valley Forge, PA: Judson Press, 1999.

Lee, Jung Young. *Korean Preaching: An Interpretation.* Nashville: Abingdon Press, 1997.

European American Preaching

Adams, Jay E. *Preaching with Purpose.* Grand Rapids, MI: Zondervan, 1986.

Allen, Ronald J. *Interpreting the Gospel: An Introduction to Preaching.* St. Louis: Chalice Press, 1998.

Bartlett, David Lyon. *Between the Bible and the Church: New Methods for Biblical Preaching.* Nashville: Abingdon Press, 1999.

Brueggman, Walter. *Finally Comes the Poet: Daring Speech for Proclamation.* Minneapolis: Fortress Press, 1989.

Buechner, Frederick. *Telling the Truth: The Gospel as Comedy, Tragedy, and Fairy Tale.* San Francisco: Harper and Row, 1978.

Buttrick, David G. *Homiletic: Moves and Structures.* Philadelphia: Fortress Press, 1987.

Claypool, John. *The Preaching Event.* Waco: Word Books, 1980.

Cox, James W., ed. *Biblical Preaching: An Expositor's Treasury.* Philadelphia: Westminster Press, 1983.

_____. *Preaching: A Comprehensive Approach to the Design and Delivery of Sermons.* San Francisco: Harper & Row Publishers, 1985.

Craddock, Fred B. *Overhearing the Gospel.* Nashville: Abingdon Press, 1978.

_____. *As One Without Authority.* Nashville: Abingdon Press, 1995.

_____. *Preaching.* Nashville: Abingdon Press, 1985.

Crum, Milton. *Manual For Preaching.* Harrisburg, PA: Morehouse Publishing Company, 1988.

Davis, H. Grady. *Design for Preaching.* Minneapolis: Augsburg Fortress Publishers, 1958.

Eslinger, Richard L. *A New Hearing: Living Options in Homiletic Method.* Nashville: Abingdon Press, 1987.

Graves, Mike. *The Sermon as Symphony: Preaching the Literary Forms of the New Testament.* Valley Forge, PA: Judson Press, 1997.

Long, Thomas G. *The Witness of Preaching,* Second Edition. Louisville: Westminster Press, 2005.

Lowry, Eugene L. *Doing Time in the Pulpit: The Relationship Between Narrative and Preaching.* Nashville: Abingdon Press, 1985.

_____. *How to Preach a Parable: Designs for Narrative Sermons.* Nashville: Abingdon Press, 1989.

_____. *The Sermon: Dancing the Edge of Mystery.* Nashville: Abingdon Press, 1997.

_____. *The Homiletical Plot, Expanded Edition: The Sermon as Narrative Art Form.* Louisville: Westminster John Knox Press, 2001.

McKenzie, Alyce M. and John C. Holbert. *What Not to Say: Avoiding the Common Mistakes that Can Sink Your Sermon.* Westminster John Knox Press, 2011.

_____. *Preaching Proverbs: Wisdom for Pulpit.* Louisville: Westminster John Knox Press, 1996.

_____. *Novel Preaching: Tips from Top Writers on Crafting Creative Sermons,* Louisville: Westminster John Knox Press, 2010.

Robinson, Wayne Bradley, ed. *Journeys Toward Narrative Preaching.* New York: Pilgrim Press, 1990.

Taylor, Barbara Brown. *The Preaching Life.* Boston: Cowley, 1993.

Troeger, Thomas H. *Imagining a Sermon.* Nashville: Abingdon Press, 1990.

Wilson, Paul Scott. *The Practice of Preaching.* Nashville: Abingdon Press, 1995.

Pastoral Preaching

Black, Kathy. *A Healing Homiletic: Preaching and Disability.* Nashville: Abingdon Pres, 1966.

Carl, William J., ed. *Graying Gracefully: Preaching to Older Adults.* Louisville: Westminster John Knox Press, 1997.

Jeter, Joseph R. *Crisis Preaching: Personal and Public.* Nashville: Abingdon Press, 1998.

McClure, John S., and Nancy J. Ramsay, eds. *Telling the Truth: Preaching about Sexual and Domestic Violence.* Cleveland, OH: United Church Press, 1998.

Ramsey, G. Lee. *Care-Full Preaching: From Sermon to Caring Community.* St. Louis: Chalice Press, 2000.

Wimberly, Edward P. *Moving from Shame to Self-Worth: Preaching and Pastoral Care.* Nashville: Abingdon Press, 1999.

Prophetic Preaching

Brueggemann, Walter. *Cadences of Home: Preaching Among Exiles.* Louisville: Westminster John Knox Press, 1997.

Burghardt, Walter J. *Preaching the Just Word.* New Haven: Yale University Press, 1996.

Gonzalez, Justo L., and Gonzalez, Catherine G. *Liberation Preaching: The Pulpit and the Oppressed.* Abingdon Preacher's Library. Nashville: Abingdon Press, 1980.

_____. *The Liberating Pulpit.* Nashville: Abingdon Press, 1994.

McMickle, Marvin A. *Where Have All the Prophets Gone? Reclaiming Prophetic Preaching in America.* Cleveland, OH: Pilgrim Press, 2006.

Resner, Andre, ed. *Just Preaching: Prophetic Voices for Economic Justice.* St. Louis: Chalice Press, 2003.

Wogaman, J. Philip. *Speaking the Truth in Love: Prophetic Preaching to a Broken World.* Louisville: Westminster John Knox Press, 1998.

Preaching on Special Occasions

Hedahl, Susan K. *Preaching the Wedding Sermon*. St. Louis: Chalice Press, 1999.

Hughes, Robert G. *A. Trumpet in Darkness: Preaching to Mourners*. Philadelphia: Fortress Press, 1985.

Feminist Preaching

Rose, Lucy A. *Sharing the Word: Preaching in the Roundtable Church*. Louisville: Westminster John Knox Press, 1997.

Smith, Christine M. *Preaching as Weeping, Confession, and Resistance: Radical Responses to Radical Evil*. Louisville: Westminster John Knox Press, 1992.

_____. *Weaving the Sermon: Preaching in a Feminist Perspective*. Louisville: Westminster John Knox Press, 1989.

Turner, Mary Donovan, and Mary Lin Hudson. *Saved from Silence: Finding Women's Voice in Preaching*. St. Louis: Chalice Press, 1999.

Womanist Preaching

Allen, Donna. "Toward a Womanist Homiletic: Katie Cannon, Alice Walker, and Emancipatory Proclamation." PhD dissertation, Vanderbilt University, 2005.

Cannon, Katie. "Womanist Interpretation and Preaching in the Black Church." *Katie's Canon: Womanism and the Soul of the Black Community*. New York: Continuum, 1995, 113-121.

_____. "Womanist Interpretation and Preaching in the Black Church." *Searching the Scriptures: A Feminist Introduction 1,* Elizabeth Fiorenza, ed. New York: Crossroad, 1993: 326-337.

_____. *Katie's Canon: Womanism and the Soul of the Black Community*. New York: Continuum, 1995.

Flake, Elaine M. *God in Her Midst: Preaching Healing to Wounded Women*. Valley Forge, PA: Judson Press, 2007.

Johnson, Kimberly Patrice. "Say 'Amen' for the Sistahs: The Rhetoric of Womanist Preaching." PhD dissertation, The University of Memphis, August 2010.

Journals

The African American Pulpit (Suspended) Homiletic
  Interpretation
  Journal for Preachers

Lectionary Homiletics

The Living Pulpit

Preaching-related websites and blogs:

- Academy of Preachers - www.academyofpreachers.net
- Center for Excellence in Preaching at Calvin Theological Seminary - http://cep.calvinseminary.edu/
- The Center for Pastoral Excellence at Christian Theological Seminary - http://www.cpx.cts.edu/

o The New Media Project

http://www.cpx.cts.edu/newmedia

This site examines how communities of faith (congregations, organizations, and institutions) and their leaders are using new media in innovative ways. The case studies, in particular, are rich with stories and interviews with pastors using technology for a variety of purposes, including preaching.

o The Academy of Preaching and Celebration under the leadership of Frank A. Thomas http://www.cpx.cts.edu/preaching

- Day1 http://day1.org

Day 1 offers over fifteen years of lectionary-based sermon transcripts, as well as audio sermons, video interviews, blog posts, and other resources for preachers and church leaders. Day 1 is in the process of expanding its website in order to offer the vast majority of sermons in audio and text that were preached between 1945-1995 on the widely heard "Protestant Hour" radio broadcast.

- Preaching blog by David Lose http://www.davidlose.net/topics/communication/preaching-communication

- Luther Seminary workingpreacher.org

- Alyce M. McKenzie
  Weekly column on the gospel lectionary text http://www.patheos.com/About-Patheos/Alyce-McKenzie.html

- Weekly blog on noticing details in daily life for preaching KnackforNoticing, http://www.patheos.com/blogs/knackfornoticing/

- "ON Scripture - The Bible" http://odysseynetworks.org/news/onscripture-the-bible Odyssey Networks produces the weekly online resource. Each week scholars connect the Common Lectionary texts for the coming weekend to current issues and Odyssey produces an accompanying video. Odyssey Network also has just begun a similar resource for the Jewish audience, "ON Scripture – The Torah."

- Peter Wallace
  Posts regularly on mainline faith and expression on HuffingtonPost.com/Religion, Patheos.com, and Day1.org.

- The Text This Week
  www.textweek.com
  Run by Jenee Woodward

This site features a wide variety of resources for study and liturgy based on the 3-year Revised Common Lectionary* cycle. Woodard writes, "I intentionally include a diverse variety of resources for scripture study, reflection, and liturgy, and purposefully do not restrict the resources to any particular theological/ideological position, including my own. The site is a work-in- progress. I spend between forty and sixty hours each week updating links and finding more resources to link."

• Western Theological Seminary http://www.westernsem.edu/journey/communities/bast-preaching-program/